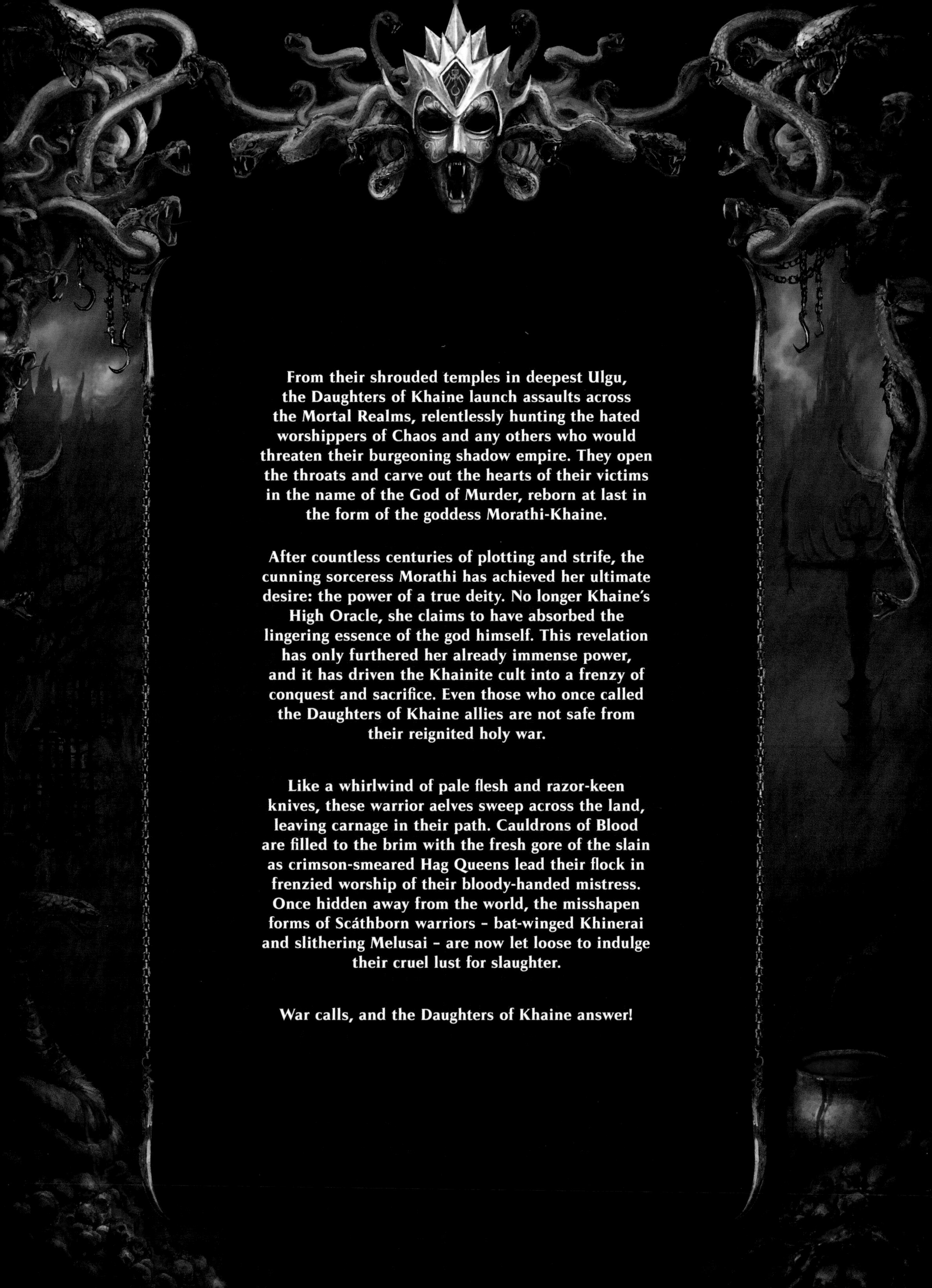

From their shrouded temples in deepest Ulgu, the Daughters of Khaine launch assaults across the Mortal Realms, relentlessly hunting the hated worshippers of Chaos and any others who would threaten their burgeoning shadow empire. They open the throats and carve out the hearts of their victims in the name of the God of Murder, reborn at last in the form of the goddess Morathi-Khaine.

After countless centuries of plotting and strife, the cunning sorceress Morathi has achieved her ultimate desire: the power of a true deity. No longer Khaine's High Oracle, she claims to have absorbed the lingering essence of the god himself. This revelation has only furthered her already immense power, and it has driven the Khainite cult into a frenzy of conquest and sacrifice. Even those who once called the Daughters of Khaine allies are not safe from their reignited holy war.

Like a whirlwind of pale flesh and razor-keen knives, these warrior aelves sweep across the land, leaving carnage in their path. Cauldrons of Blood are filled to the brim with the fresh gore of the slain as crimson-smeared Hag Queens lead their flock in frenzied worship of their bloody-handed mistress. Once hidden away from the world, the misshapen forms of Scáthborn warriors - bat-winged Khinerai and slithering Melusai - are now let loose to indulge their cruel lust for slaughter.

War calls, and the Daughters of Khaine answer!

CONTENTS

PRODUCED BY THE WARHAMMER STUDIO

With thanks to The Faithful for their additional playtesting services.

British Cataloguing-in-Publication Data. A catalogue record for this book is available from the British Library. Pictures used for illustrative purposes only.

Games Workshop Ltd., Willow Road, Lenton, Nottingham, NG7 2WS, United Kingdom

games-workshop.com

Filled with a bitter hatred of all who worship the Dark Gods, the monstrous entity known as the Shadow Queen leads a war coven of Hagg Nar in pursuit of holy slaughter.

DAUGHTERS OF KHAINE

They crave battle and seek power through bloodshed, honouring their deity with every kill. Even their closest allies shudder to witness the gory rituals that renew and reinvigorate these graceful murderers. They are the Daughters of Khaine, and to cross blades with them is to invite death.

The Daughters of Khaine move with quicksilver speed, carving into enemies like a whirlwind of steel. As blades flash, the she-aelves shed their visage of cold and distant beauty, their ecstatic faces alight with each fresh kill. To them, the clash of arms is the height of their religion – holy rites practised and perfected with all the considerable skill and grace of aelfkind. As blood is spilled, shrill dedications to Khaine ring out, and with each gore-splattered offering, the Daughters rapturously grow in power and fury. In their frenzy, Khaine's worshippers are closest to their divinity, invigorated by his iron-hearted spirit and insatiable bloodlust.

True to their merciless god, the Daughters of Khaine continue the slaughter until every last foe has fallen. Khaine, the ancient aelven god of battle and bloodshed, was said to have been destroyed by the Chaos Gods – a claim vehemently denied by the matriarchal cult. Indeed, to speak such heresy is a crime punishable by death – a sentence that the militant order prosecutes with extreme zeal.

Devotees of Khaine are amongst the most ferocious warriors in all the realms. Echoing the single-minded focus of their god, they have devoted their entire existence to the mastery of battle, serving the Bloody-Handed One in the only fitting fashion: by offering a mighty tribute of blood and slaughtered foes. For these fierce souls, there is no satisfaction beyond the thrill of feeling their blades slice through flesh and bone.

The highly matriarchal Khainite society is entirely structured around the twin pillars of war and worship. Females dedicate themselves to combat training and the observance of gruesome religious rites, while a caste of male serfs known as leathanam carry out such tasks as their masters deem to be beneath them, freeing the Daughters of Khaine to concentrate on more worthy goals. A life of ceaseless gladiatorial combat and battle hones the natural grace of the aelves to near supernatural levels, ensuring that even the lowest-ranking Witch Aelf possesses formidable martial prowess and the boldness of one to whom bloody combat is as natural as breathing.

Most feared of all Khainites are the Scáthborn, half-aelven creatures fashioned from dark sorcery with the bodies of serpents or winged nightmares. These cold-blooded killers rarely stray outside the confines of their hidden lairs, emerging only when war calls. In such times, they join the Khainite hosts as elite soldiers, displaying not a hint of mercy as they lay waste to their prey.

SACRED BLADES

During the Age of Myth, aelves of any kind were difficult to find; however, hidden within the shadowy realm of Ulgu, the Daughters of Khaine flourished. With Sigmar's re-opening of Azyr, the growing cult spread still further. The Daughters have built shrines to Khaine in nearly all of the great settlements founded since the coming of the Age of Sigmar, although each of the rival sects names the seminal temple-city of Hagg Nar as the capital of their violent creed.

Yet the Daughters of Khaine are not content with these impressive holdings; they seek to spread the influence of their warlike god to all corners of the realms. As their battle pilgrimages range into enemy lands and throngs of zealous worshippers seek to subvert the governance of their supposed allies, the power of the Khainites continues to surge.

The faith itself has diverged into several powerful sects, each of which venerates a different aspect of Khaine's bloodthirsty nature. The blademasters of Draichi Ganeth worship Khaine as the executioner and seek to honour him through mastery of the killing blow, while the nomadic Khailebron revere his aspect as the unseen assassin striking from the shadows.

The Daughters of Khaine are a mysterious order, hated by their foes and misunderstood and often feared by their allies. However, none who have fought beside them would ever deny that they were staunch enemies of Chaos. When Alarielle, Everqueen of the Sylvaneth, called for aid to reclaim her realm of Ghyran from the diseased grip of Nurgle's plague legions, none answered the call to battle with more zeal than did the Khainite cult.

It is not the corrupted alone who feel the Daughters' wrath, for countless foes and monsters have fallen before their blades. When the orruks of Grokhold threatened the newly raised city of Kurnothea, it was the Daughters of Khaine who stood shoulder to shoulder with the Stormcast Eternals to safeguard the burgeoning civilisation.

Yet despite their undoubted heroics, the Daughters have won little trust. Claims of extreme savagery and allegations of gruesome rituals and snake-bodied mutants give pause to even their most ardent supporters. Indeed, even those who have long held a profitable and secure alliance with Hagg Nar now look upon the Khainite sects with deep suspicion. Rumours abound of bloody coups and uprisings in distant lands, and those who raise the ire of the zealous aelves have a habit of meeting a violent end.

THE SHADOW QUEEN

A single being stands behind the unlikely revitalisation of a fallen people and the promulgation of a fading religion: the infamous Morathi. A living legend who predates the Age of Myth, Morathi is an aelven sorceress whose eldritch mastery is rivalled by few beings in all the realms. Her past is interwoven with countless schemes, falls from grace and unexpected triumphs, and legends have spread far and wide of her great beauty and cunning.

For a long time, Morathi claimed to be the High Oracle of Khaine, the only living conduit to the warlike deity's will. She used her influence and talent for manipulation to grow the cult of Khaine from a fractured sisterhood into a realms-spanning power. Now Hagg Nar is truly a force to be reckoned with, a thriving city-state populated by fervent warriors who dedicate their entire lives to the mastery of battle. Yet even this was not enough to sate Morathi's ambition.

In a ritual of dark sorcery, Morathi tore free and consumed a clutch of mighty souls from the belly of the captive Slaanesh, finally attaining the divinity that had long eluded her. But success did not come without a cost. During the ritual, Morathi's very being was sundered, cleaved in body and spirit by the overwhelming energies being channelled. Thus was the sorceress divided into two separate forms united by a common consciousness: the wise and regal Voice of Khaine and the macabre monstrosity known as the Shadow Queen, an embodiment of all Morathi's rage and bitterness.

Despite the unexpected outcome, Morathi had achieved that which she had sought for so long. Thus empowered, she proclaimed herself Morathi-Khaine – the Bloody-Handed God remade in the flesh. Flushed with new-found power, Morathi will not be satisfied until all bow before her, until every slight she has ever suffered is repaid in kind, until she takes her rightful place as the unquestioned master of the Mortal Realms.

Morathi understands the power of tradition and ancient custom well, and she has been careful not to tear apart the foundations of the faith. Many Khainites still venerate the Bloody-Handed God in his traditional, masculine aspect, reciting the ancient battle rites and performing rituals in his honour. Yet slowly but surely, Morathi is reshaping the religion that she herself created to better suit her whims – and her ego. Towering effigies depicting the goddess in all her regal beauty are beginning to replace the old depictions of Khaine, and texts that have endured for centuries are being subtly altered by her High Priestesses to secure Morathi's legacy and alter history in her favour. After so many centuries of masquerading as Khaine's prophet, Morathi grows weary of standing behind the throne. She is a goddess now, after all.

This has not gone entirely unnoticed. There are whispers of Khainite hardliners who have voiced heretical concerns as to the former High Oracle of Khaine's motives. Yet with Morathi's utterly loyal Scáthborn maintaining a ceaseless vigil across the Khainite temples and using disguise and illusion to keep close watch on any who show even a flicker of dissent, any organised objection to the divinity of Morathi-Khaine has thus far been ruthlessly extinguished. For now, at least, the Khainite cult retains its adamant unity, and with every day, Morathi's influence – already near-total – grows even stronger.

For all her vaulting ambitions, Morathi is no fool. Hagg Nar's enemies are many, and the Daughters of Khaine cannot fight them all alone. Her conquest will be one of subtle manipulation as much as all-out war, a shadow campaign in which supposed allies are set against one another and enemies are tricked into carrying out the Shadow Queen's will. The Khainite sects stand ready to seize every possible opportunity.

BLOOD MAGIC

Morathi's ascension to godhood has granted her untold power, and she is only just beginning to test the boundaries of her new abilities. To the High Priestesses of the Daughters of Khaine, one of the surest signs of the Bloody-Handed God's reincarnation is the sudden surge in divine might that each has experienced.

Invoked by incantation and sacrifice, the blazing manifestation known as a Heart of Fury has appeared in the skies above many a Khainite war coven, stirring all who look upon it into a delirious frenzy that allows them to shrug off the gravest injuries. The enemies of Hagg Nar have learnt to dread this omen, for it heralds terrible bloodshed. For seven days and nights, such an icon hung over the Tzeentchian citadel of Tallizca, bathing the silver city in a crimson light as an inferno of sorcery and bloodshed swept through its labyrinthine streets. That time of blood resulted in the gruesome deaths of each and every member of the Arcanite Cult of the Twistgyre, all of whom were drained of their blood and staked to the walls of their once mighty citadel.

Many Khainite battle prayers gain their strength from Morathi's own divine essence, but the ruler of Hagg Nar has also granted her most trusted sorcerers the knowledge to cast new and terrible arcane conjurations of her own devising. These spellcasters have exulted in bringing forth the Bladewind – whirling falchions that scythe through the enemy in an eruption of gore.

Perhaps more terrifying still is the Bloodwrack Viper. Summoned from the bubbling blood of a sacrificial cauldron, this coiling, serpentine monstrosity smothers the caster's foes in a scalding embrace. This is a particular favourite of Morathi's loyal Medusae, for the spell calls upon the malicious curse that runs through their veins – and those of the Shadow Queen.

The Daughters of Khaine are on the rise. Driven to new heights of zealotry by the reincarnation of their wrathful deity, they seek to expand the borders of their shadow empire across the realms – and they will make a bloody

DANCING WITH SHADOWS

Nurtured in secrecy behind veils of shadow, the Daughters of Khaine have expanded from a small murder-cult of aelves clinging to an ancient religion into a major power. In those earliest of days, the cult, like Morathi herself, seemed doomed to dwindle – or to disappear altogether.

Morathi awoke early in the Age of Myth. After being captured in a nightmare, she found herself hurtling downwards through grey clouds. Her descent from heights unknown ended in an explosion of steam as Morathi impacted the Umbralic Sea. Only her mastery of magic saved the sorceress, who found herself alone in a conjured sphere of protection, bobbing on the surface of a dismal ocean. She had come to rest in Ulgu, the Realm of Shadow, a land of mists and misdirection, where illusion and lies hung as heavily as fog.

How long Morathi wandered that darksome place she did not recall, but slowly she began to tap into the arcane energies of Ulgu. A master of dark sorcery, Morathi was naturally adept at wielding this new force. She needed it, for there was a time when she had traded blood sacrifices to Khaine in exchange for her youthful vigour and appearance. Such offerings had ceased to work. While Morathi's mind had teetered back into a fragile sanity, her body had not – her form was no longer aelven but that of some misshapen serpentine monster. It was reminiscent of Chaos and her tormentor, and such thoughts caused the sorceress great anguish.

Desperate for companionship, Morathi found only gloom. Using her magics, she conjured forth spirits from the hidden places – mist elementals and shadow daemons. Morathi could not tell how much time she spent in the company of these entities, but with them she explored the wide expanses of those mysterious lands. She travelled all thirteen of the vast regions of Ulgu, uncovering innumerable secrets. During her journeys, Morathi encountered many strange beings, yet she met none of her own kind. The horror experienced by other creatures upon meeting her was a constant reminder of the ugliness that had wormed its way deep into her soul. Bitter were Morathi's tears, for vanity had ever been her greatest failing. By bending the illusionary and shapeshifting magics of shadow to her will and using the secrets whispered by her by her shadow-daemon consorts, Morathi attempted to regain her old form. She swallowed coils of penumbral magic and transformed into a semblance of her previous incarnation. It was in this aelven form that her path crossed that of her son, Malerion. No joy came from the reunion of mother and child, for both nursed ancient resentments. Furthermore, Morathi was beside herself with bitterness, for Malerion was imbued with immense power. That he had gained immortality and an even greater affinity with the shadows than Morathi was only too apparent. Despite their mutual misgivings, each sought to join forces in the hope of finding other aelves in these new lands.

So it was that when Sigmar's journeys brought him to Ulgu, he found Malerion and Morathi working together. They had used their magics to raise up a great citadel – the foundations of Druchiroth, the ruling seat for the largest of the thirteen kingdoms of Ulgu. Sigmar aided them and, in turn, they joined his Pantheon of Order – a growing alliance that united many disparate gods, titanic beasts and beings of great power. In this way, Morathi and Malerion helped bring civilisation to each of the Mortal Realms, fostering cities and teaching the arcane arts to primitive peoples. Few aelves were discovered, however, and most of these settled in the celestial city of Azyrheim.

During their time in the pantheon, neither Malerion nor Morathi were fully trusted, though where her son drew praise for his help, Morathi was ostracised. While Tyrion and Teclis – the rulers of the Realm of Light – found common cause with Malerion, neither would deign to work alongside one whom they considered tainted. This reticence – along with her lingering reputation for treachery and double-dealing – caused many to shun Morathi. So it was that she left the Great Alliance and sought to establish her own dwellings in Ulgu. Malerion outright rejected her suggestion of splitting the rule of the Thirteen Dominions, for he claimed all the Shadowlands as his own. Her protests were met with scorn until, either as a jest or as a plot to rid himself of her, Malerion granted his mother a small parcel of land in the middle of the Umbral Veil. This was perhaps the darkest and most impenetrable of all the regions, and none save himself had ever returned from those cloying mists with their sanity intact.

In this, Malerion underestimated his mother. Morathi bent the shadows into a protective shroud around her new land. Her only followers were the aelven witch-cults that maintained their worship of Khaine. To ensure their loyalty, Morathi built a temple to Khaine, naming it Hagg Nar, and taught them the secrets of navigating the murky currents. Hagg Nar began as a pitiful kingdom, outshone by the wonders of Sigmar's growing empire and the dark majesty of Druchiroth. Morathi's frustration was great. She sought power and status, yet there seemed little opportunity to gain either in this dark corner of the realms. Her followers were few and clung dogmatically to a faith that Morathi felt was misplaced – she believed the old gods dead, for she no longer felt their power. Yet this nadir of despair proved a turning point. She was not going be content to fade away in a hidden demesne bereft of glory, nor would she merely manipulate others from behind the throne. She would forsake her old ways and rely upon no one but herself.

THE POWER OF AELF-SOULS

Slaanesh may have crept away into hiding after feasting at will during the death of the World-that-Was, but he could not conceal the cries of tormented aelf-souls echoing from his belly from the aelven gods. Eager to reclaim the essences of their lost kin, the aelven gods Teclis, Tyrion and Malerion created a plan to lure Slaanesh out of hiding and into Uhl-Gysh, the Hidden Gloaming – a no-place that existed between the realms of Hysh and Ulgu. So desperate were the three that they recruited Morathi, for they needed a balance of light and shadow magic, and they suspected she had hidden knowledge of Slaanesh.

Teclis had surmised correctly that Morathi herself had once been trapped within Slaanesh. That information, along with the tale of how she escaped, would be needed, for the aelven gods hoped not only to punish Slaanesh for what he had done but also to extract the swallowed souls that were still imprisoned within the depraved god. Reluctantly, Morathi shared her horrific memories for the first and only time. She spoke of her suffering and how she had caused the Dark Prince to vomit her back into reality. Armed with that knowledge, arcane preparations were made on a vast scale, and the energies of both the realms of Hysh and Ulgu were harnessed as never before.

The full tale of the mystical battles that followed is long and harrowing, but the end result was this: using themselves as bait, the aelven gods, Morathi and several cabals of sorcerers succeeded both in entrapping Slaanesh and in beginning the slow process of extracting aelven souls from the Chaos God. The monumental deed could not have been done without the aid of Morathi's sorcery and the vile wisdoms garnered from her own grim experience in the god's belly.

Before long, the freed souls of captured aelves were streaming back into the Mortal Realms. In return for her indispensable aid, Morathi had also demanded a share of reclaimed souls. The Máthcoir, an immense iron cauldron, was created as a place to store Morathi's newly claimed energies.

There, beneath the temple of Hagg Nar, Morathi used enchantments, sacrificial power, raw shadow magic and her own blood to help whisper into existence new and suitable forms for these reclaimed souls. Thus were the first Melusai and Khinerai born. They became Morathi's Handmaidens and aided in all her new endeavours. They alone were allowed in the underhall of Khruthú. All of Hagg Nar was filled with the sounds of blood rituals to fuel the city's expansion.

ULGU BESIEGED

Morathi sought followers and power; through her own works, she found both. At the end of the Age of Myth, even as the civilisations of the Mortal Realms were threatened by the coming of Chaos, a new force was building strength within the mist-shrouded lands of Ulgu.

Where once Morathi had been ambivalent about the worship of Khaine, she now dedicated herself with righteous fury to the ancient god. Indeed, Morathi claimed that the god of battle, cruelty and murder had spoken to her, naming her as his High Oracle. She was to be a conduit for Khaine, a leader who would speak in his voice. Morathi revealed that Khaine had indeed fought the Chaos Gods and had been broken into fragments, but he was regaining power thanks to his worshippers. Witch Aelves were sent to scour the Mortal Realms for any signs of the shards of Khaine. Only through sacrifice and worship could the fractured god be made whole.

The reclamation of souls from Slaanesh heralded a new age for all members of the aelven race, and the Daughters of Khaine flourished. Within a few generations, they were no longer a dwindling cult. Hagg Nar grew from a temple stronghold to a shrine-filled city and then to a city-state – a Khainite nation hidden within the mistfields. However, it was soon overcrowded, and new problems beset Morathi, for it had always been the way of Khaine that the weak died or bowed their knee to the strong. The aelven males were sufficiently cowed – indeed, they were made that way – but rivalries between would-be Hag Queens flared up as they fought for supremacy within the Witch Aelf hierarchy. The maxim of survival of the fittest was fine up to a point, but Morathi did not wish to see her growing armies tear themselves apart.

Her remedy was to declare more shard-quests and to send enclaves to found entire new temple-colonies. The beginnings of new sects were established during this time, each separatist Hag Queen and her followers fixating upon an aspect of Khaine's worship, such as single combat, assassination or unchecked slaughter. Most built their own temples, but some embarked on an eternal pilgrimage in honour of Khaine. All still bowed before the High Oracle, for Morathi spoke with a voice of iron; to all Daughters, Morathi's words were still law.

Although the Daughters of Khaine were growing in power, not all was well with the Mortal Realms. While the aelven gods focused their energies upon their elaborate trap and the recouping of their lost kin, Sigmar's pantheon had fractured, and familiar mortal sins began to fester within his teeming cities. The Dark Gods, primordial foes of mortalkind, exploited these weaknesses in order to create

breaches in reality through which to spill their daemonic legions. So did the Age of Myth collapse and the Age of Chaos begin.

THE CATHTRAR DHULE

Daemons spilled across reality, burning and slaughtering. Age-old kingdoms were torn down to the last stone, their populace devoured in a gory bacchanal. Separated and splintered by their own rivalries, the Pantheon of Order proved easy prey.

Hagg Nar soon stood alone. While Sigmar, Nagash and the other members of the pantheon were condemned to a crushing rout by the forces of Archaon the Everchosen, Morathi took great pride in the fact that her shadowy domain was never conquered. Experts in lightning ambush and merciless guerrilla war, the Daughters of Khaine fought a bloody, centuries-long conflict against the encroaching armies of Chaos, foremost amongst them the great hosts of Slaanesh. The Dark Prince's followers did not know the truth of what had happened to their foul deity, but they could smell the perfumed scent of his spoor throughout Ulgu. Known by Khainites as the Cathtrar Dhule, this terrible time of bloodshed and strife claimed a vast number of aelven lives. Yet Morathi's peerless strategy and her warriors' mastery of the ever-shifting and treacherous wilds of the Umbral Veil proved decisive. Hagg Nar itself was besieged more than once, but it never fell – a fact about which the Shadow Queen is not shy to remind her rivals.

Even so, Morathi held no illusions about her good fortune. Her shadow empire had perched upon the edge of a precipice and would surely have been consumed, had not the God-King sent forth his Stormcast Eternals to meet the hosts of Chaos in battle and forever changed the balance of power in the Mortal Realms. Morathi was quick to make common cause with Sigmar, despite the fact that she held no great regard for the God-King, considering him a simple-minded brute with ideas above his station. Nevertheless, the coming of the mighty hosts of the heavens granted beleaguered Hagg Nar a welcome reprieve.

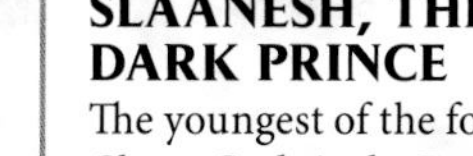

SLAANESH, THE DARK PRINCE

The youngest of the four greater Chaos Gods is the Dark Prince, Slaanesh, the Lord of Pleasure. While Slaanesh hungers for the souls of all mortals, he finds those of aelfkind the most enticing. With their heightened senses and depth of emotion, aelves have the greatest capacity for empathy and discipline – and also for decadence and depravity. Such heights of obsession are the finest delicacy to Slaanesh.

Following the destruction of the World-that-Was, the Dark Prince went missing. This was no accident, for the god had hidden himself, hoping to digest his overindulgent feast upon millions of aelven souls. Alas, despite his best efforts, the Dark Prince could not hide from the all-illuminating light of Teclis. Through the trickery and magic of the aelven gods, Slaanesh was lured out from his dwelling and trapped. The vulnerable god was bound in paradoxical chains and – with the aid of Malerion and Morathi – slowly bled of the souls on which he had gorged.

Of all her many enemies, Morathi reserves the greatest portion of her hatred for Slaanesh, for it was he that captured her following the death of the World-that-Was. The sufferings she experienced at the Dark Prince's hands continue to torment her to this day, and now that she possesses divinity herself, she is intent upon repaying them a thousand fold.

Ironically, Morathi's recent ascension to godhood granted Slaanesh a taste of power such as he had not known for centuries – a fact that would surely fill the leader of the Daughters of Khaine with bile, were she aware of the truth.

THE ORACLE'S GAMBIT

With the Mortal Realms rocked by the Shyish Necroquake and her rivals distracted by the wars and magical storms ravaging their territories, Morathi saw her chance to reach for glory. She put into motion a plot centuries in the making – a scheme of astonishing ambition and scope.

For many years after Sigmar's return to the Mortal Realms, Morathi was content to turn her power to the cause of Order. Her agents gladly welcomed the opportunity to take their place in the God-King's rapidly developing free cities, and the sight of a foreboding Khainite shrine or bloodstained gladiatorial arena echoing to the shrieked mantras of Witch Aelves was not entirely uncommon in otherwise human-dominated metropolises. Khainites were feared and mistrusted for their barbarity, sure enough, but none questioned their hatred of Chaos, nor their bravery in battle. Indeed, the elite forces of Hagg Nar, Draichi Ganeth and other sects fought and bled alongside the Stormcast Eternals and their mortal auxiliaries.

In the aftermath of the Shyish Necroquake and the outright assault upon civilisation by Nagash's undead legions, the Daughters of Khaine once again proved deadly allies. Morathi herself visited cities such as the mighty Hammerhal, sowing the seeds of alliances that would be invaluable to both parties. There was no altruism on Morathi's part. The coalition of Hagg Nar and Azyr was a means to an end – a necessary if distasteful compromise that would protect the interests of Hagg Nar while the High Oracle pursued other, greater endeavours out of sight of her supposed allies.

THE ULTIMATE PRIZE

Divinity is not something easily attained. The great deities of the realms each earned their godly power through strife and struggle over the span of millennia. Most were mortal once, save of course bestial Gorkamorka and the Chaos Gods, those manifestations of unrestrained passion and emotion that dwell within the Realm of Chaos. Some sought godhood out with feverish intensity. Others had it thrust upon them, a burden they gladly accepted in order to better serve their people. For Morathi, the search for godhood was deeply personal. She had spent a lifetime on the periphery of true power, advising and observing, pulling the strings from the shadows. For a time, this sufficed. But after the horrors she experienced at the hands of Slaanesh, and the scorn with which her aelven kin received her, Morathi swore that never again would she bow and scrape before another. She would become a god and unlock the paths to true power that had always remained sealed to her.

THE STUFF OF CHANGE

As the Soul Wars tore across the realms, Morathi bided her time, allowing her greatest rivals to bleed each other while reserving her own power. Khainite war covens did rally to the cause of her allies, of course, and the Realm of Shadow was in no way immune to the predations of the Great Necromancer; however, Morathi cunningly avoided the worst of the fighting while simultaneously building trust with the God-King and Alarielle the Everqueen by sending detachments to protect their ravaged empires.

It was at this time of great upheaval that Morathi sensed the opportunity she had been waiting for. Word reached the court of Hagg Nar that a vast deposit of varanite had been discovered beneath the infernal forge of Varanthax's Maw. This strange, molten realmstone was of great interest to Morathi; she had heard rumours of its ability to remake flesh and bone, to twist the physical form of those exposed to it into terrible new shapes. Varanite was vanishingly rare, only found in the Eightpoints, that island sub-realm that lay in the centre of the cosmos and was claimed by Archaon the Everchosen as his personal stronghold.

Varanite was raw and lethal Chaos magic given physical form. Few wielders of the arcane would have anything to do with such a substance, but Morathi had dabbled in forbidden sorceries before, and she recognised its raw potentiality in samples recovered by her Shadowstalker agents at great expense. If it could be tempered somehow, its warping energies controlled and refined, then varanite possessed the power to change the flesh and the soul entirely. With sufficient quantities, the Shadow Queen might be able to alter her own monstrous, serpentine form.

Moreover, molten realmstone would provide the perfect catalyst for Morathi's ultimate goal: the completion of a ritual of complex and far-reaching consequence that would finally secure her path to godhood. Varanite alone, however, would not suffice. Her ambitious plans involved seeking out long-lost souls, and to do this, she required an artefact of legendary power and ancient provenance.

Of all the countless wonders crafted by the mage-lord Teclis, few rival the Ocarian Lantern for their sheer wonder and beauty. Woven from the tapestry of Hysh by the aelven god's dexterous magic, the Lantern blazed with the purest radiance, a cleansing light so powerful that it could summon lost souls from the aether. Teclis had used the radiant light of this magical device to draw forth tortured aelf-spirits from Slaanesh's gut and remake them in the image of ancient aelven glory.

The Lantern had been stolen away from Teclis by his own creations: the Cythai, forebears of the Idoneth Deepkin. The mysterious creatures of the dark oceans feared destruction at the hands of their maker, for Teclis considered them a failed experiment and sensed in them a coldness and cruelty that he wished to expunge. And so they took the Ocarian Lantern with them when they fled beneath the waves, ensuring its illuminating beams could not be used to seek them out. Yet they did not reckon with the spies and agents of Morathi.

The Idoneth had hidden the artefact in the plunging abyss known as the Sarr Danoi, in a temple guarded by hideous monsters of the deep. The aelves thought this resting place impenetrable, but they had reckoned without the skill of Morathi's elite Shadowstalkers. The winding strands of the Umbral Web stretched even into the Sarr Danoi, and from that realm-spanning passage crept a host of dark figures. Shielded from the crushing depths of the abyss by sorcerous enchantments, the Shadow Queen's agents breached the cyclopean temple at the bottom of the great chasm and – at great cost – seized the Ocarian Lantern for their master.

While this grand larceny was being committed, Morathi was weaving plans of another kind.

INTO THE EIGHTPOINTS

The presence of such vast quantities of varanite in the Maw offered Morathi not only the sorcerous fuel for her ritual but also a way to bolster her own armies with powerful allies. She personally took audience with Sigmar the God-King, bringing to the palace of Sigmaron news of Archaon's discovery – and of the dark purpose to which the Everchosen was turning his industrial might. Archaon desired to warp and twist the Meteoric Gate – the great Arcway leading to Azyr that had for so long remained impenetrable to his armies.

Alarmed at the ramifications of a direct and open route between Azyr and the Chaos-dominated Eightpoints, Sigmar agreed to dispatch an invasion force into the Everchosen's stronghold, intending to destroy the varanite at its source and delay – or perhaps even put a definitive end to – his old enemy's plans.

Morathi and her Daughters of Khaine marched alongside the God-King's army, since it was she who had proposed the radical plot to destroy the varanite. Her plan was to summon a vortex to the aetheric void with the aid of Stormcast wizards, a breach in reality through which the varanite would drain away into nothingness. Of course, Morathi had no intention of doing any such thing. Through misdirection and subterfuge, the High Oracle allowed her Sigmarite allies to keep the Chaos defenders of the Maw occupied while she and her elite Zainthar Kai formations made for the so-called 'Molten Wound', the sulphurous abscess deep beneath Varanthax's Maw from which raw varanite was gushing forth.

It was now that Morathi enacted her first grand betrayal, using illusions and shadowy obfuscations to conceal her true purpose. Utilising the rolling war shrines known as Blood Cauldrons – each of which was magically linked to the Mother Cauldron of Hagg Nar – Morathi claimed vast quantities of the molten realmstone. She then fled the Eightpoints, leaving her Stormcast allies isolated and surrounded on all sides by encroaching Chaos forces. She made with all haste for Hagg Nar, her island fortress in the midst of the Umbral Veil, and there began to prepare for her most important ritual. Thus far, all had progressed exactly as the High Oracle desired. But her underhanded actions had not gone unnoticed.

Though her Shadowstalkers had succeeded in stealing away the Ocarian Lantern, one of their number had been captured by the artefact's Idoneth guardians. High King Volturnos, last of the Cythai and ruler of the Idoneth enclaves, was filled with a cold anger at the High Oracle's arrogant act. More than this, the High King knew that should the Ocarian Lantern ever return to the hands of his creator, Teclis, then his people would never again find sanctuary beneath the waves. The only answer was war.

The undersea host raised by Volturnos was like none the realms had seen for centuries. As the scattered enclaves sent forth their finest Akhelian commanders to lay siege to Hagg Nar and retrieve their stolen relic, it seemed as if the ocean itself had come to life. Volturnos himself rode at the fore of this enormous deep-sea host, riding atop his noble steed Uasall.

Morathi was not caught unawares; no army, not even a force of the furtive Deepkin, could breach the borders of her lands without the High Oracle's foreknowledge. Morathi had already summoned her own armies to protect Hagg Nar. The defenders comprised not solely the combined might of a Caillich Coven, a gathering of warriors from all the Khainite sects, but also Scourge Privateers and Freeguilders from the free city of Misthåvn. The latter held no particular love for Morathi, of course, but the High Oracle had been generous in her offers of gold and treasure; the mercenary folk of the City of Scoundrels did not much care about the nature of their cause as long as their galleons' holds were filled with booty. Their firepower would prove vital in the terrible naval battles to come.

MORATHI ASCENDANT

As the forces of the Idoneth converged upon Hagg Nar from all sides, Morathi knew that time was running out. There was no retreating from this moment – she would either fulfil her greatest desire and ascend to godhood, or her empire of shadow would crumble and fall.

The Idoneth fell upon Hagg Nar like a crashing tidal wave. Immense sea beasts broke the surface of the shadowsea, smashing galleons and reaver-ships into kindling. Namarti poured onto the jagged bays that surrounded the island city-state in their thousands and were met by a screaming counter-charge from throngs of outraged Witch Aelves. As the battle raged, Morathi enacted her grand ritual.

Grasping the Ocarian Lantern in one hand and Khaine's Iron Heart in the other, she descended into the depths of the Mother Cauldron. The Máthcoir had been transformed into a conduit between Hagg Nar and the gullet of Slaanesh, and as the molten varanite boiled away her flesh, Morathi held out the Ocarian Lantern and let its radiant light shine forth. She sought souls of tremendous power, those king-souls that still lingered within the Dark Prince's roiling belly. Drawn to the lantern's light like shimmerfish to a lure, they came forth to meet their saviour. And Morathi, transforming into a horror of shadow and scaly coils, bared her fangs and began to devour them.

Yet even as she felt the stirring of untold power, Morathi's plan was at the point of unravelling. High King Volturnos and his host had forced a landing at Hagganal Bay, and even the united might of the Khainite sects could not seem to throw back their advance. Closer and closer they drew to Khruthú, the seat of Morathi's power.

Relief came from a most unexpected front. Cloying clouds of incense and agonised screams of pleasure and pain came rippling across the water as a great host of Slaaneshi Hedonites appeared on the horizon. Their swift-moving quadriremes smashed into the rear of the Idoneth host, much to the surprise of the Daughters of Khaine, who had surely expected themselves to be the hated Chaos-worshippers' quarry. Unbeknownst to the defenders of Hagg Nar, the Slaaneshi Herald Glavia Sinheart had been granted prophetic visions of the coming of a new entity – a holy servant of the Dark Prince who would be born beneath the glare of a crimson moon this bloody night.

So it was that Volturnos was forced to divide his army to face the new threat. Half of his force fought a desperate last stand to keep the Slaaneshi host at bay, while he and his finest Akhelian champions pushed on towards the heart of Hagg Nar. Though the royal host suffered grievous losses from the ruthless ambushes of Melusai and swooping packs of Khinerai, they forced their way into Khruthú in time to hear the piercing cries of Morathi and see the Mother Cauldron splinter and erupt in an explosion of scalding blood. Khainite and Idoneth alike were sent hurtling through the air by the force of the magical eruption.

MORATHI-KHAINE

As the combatants staggered to their feet, a lone figure emerged from the bloody mists: the High Oracle Morathi, still regally beautiful despite the blood that stained her alabaster skin. From behind her, another being emerged, gigantic and serpentine. Most of those present gasped in horror, for they had never seen such a monstrous creature before. But the High Oracle raised a hand and caressed the Shadow Queen's scaled flank. Morathi's smile was one of cruel triumph. After so many years of plotting and preparation, Morathi had crossed the threshold of divinity and emerged a goddess. She was Morathi-Khaine, the Bloody-Handed God reborn anew.

Volturnos, of course, cared nothing for such grand pronouncements. Cursing Morathi as a thief, he and his champions surged forwards to slay her. But divine power now coursed through Morathi's veins, and even the High King was overmatched. After a brief but furious fight, he was smashed from the back of his Deepmare and found the tip of the shadow monster's oversized spear against his throat.

Volturnos prepared to meet his death. Yet Morathi had other ideas in mind. She ordered her forces to fall back from the bloodied Deepkin landing force and gestured for her Melusai to release those Akhelians who still lived. She then spoke to the Last of the Cythai, acknowledging her crimes and offering him great recompense as a show of her contrition. Hagg Nar and the Idoneth need not be foes, she said. Both were outcasts, despised and mistrusted by their own kin. An alliance between shadow and sea would serve both their ends far better than a pointless, bloody war.

As a token of her good faith, she returned the Ocarian Lantern, splintered and cracked but still potent in its magic. Furthermore, she presented Volturnos with a most unexpected gift – the souls of many of his fellow Cythai, long thought lost to Chaos but now recovered from the belly of Slaanesh. There would be more souls, she promised. Mortal souls, in numbers great enough to recover the Idoneth losses sustained in the battle for Hagg Nar.

For many proud aelven kings, honour would have demanded that this offer of peace be scorned. However, the High King was a cold and calculating creature of the deep ocean, age-old and unfathomably wise. He saw promise in the union Morathi offered, and it stirred even his icy heart to see the spirits of his long-dead kin returned. He could not trust this self-proclaimed goddess, of course, but perhaps their causes might align – for now, at least.

THE FALL OF ANVILGARD

Flushed with the power of divinity, Morathi now sought to expand the influence of her empire beyond the borders of the Realm of Shadow. It was time to seize the moment. Yet she knew she must be careful to ensure that her reach did not exceed her grasp. Hagg Nar's next move must be decisive – not rash.

Thus, she turned her gaze to the port city of Anvilgard. Situated on the Charrwind Coast in Aqshy, on the shores of the deadly but prosperous Searing Sea, the city had long been a haven for aelvenkind. It was also a burgeoning stronghold of the Khainite faith – something that Morathi herself had been keen to subtly encourage, much to the consternation of the city's Sigmar-worshipping faithful. Not only was Anvilgard a major naval power, it was also strategically invaluable: at the centre of the city rose the Stormkeep known as the Black Nexus, a stronghold of the Anvils of the Heldenhammer. This immense, magically protected fortress was constructed around no fewer than four realmgates, each leading to a different location in the Great Parch. In short, its seizure would grant Morathi a lucrative and important centre of power in Aqshy, a stepping stone from which to plan further conquests.

Moreover, the shadowy cabal known as the Blackscale Coil had agents scattered throughout the city – agents who answered to Morathi alone. These included powerful Black Ark Fleetmasters, thousands-strong hosts of the Darkling Covens and many zealots of the Khainite faith. Command of these insurrectionists fell to the sorceress Drusa Kraeth, one of Morathi's most accomplished spies and leader of the mighty Coven of the Serpent's Blood.

The battle for Anvilgard, when it came, was short but exceedingly brutal. The Idoneth aided the insurrectionists, shrouding Anvilgard in the cloying mists of the ethersea, isolating it from the outside world and covering the movements of Morathi's traitorous armies. When the latter struck, they achieved total surprise over the outmatched and outnumbered Freeguild forces. Most were slain, their souls then reaped by the Deepkin forces lurking outside the city. Despite the heroism of Lord-Veritant Keiser Ven Brecht and his fellow Anvils of the Heldenhammer, the city fell swiftly. Every Stormcast warrior was taken alive, having been brought down with poisoned bolts and mind-scouring magic – Morathi did not wish any to die, lest they return to Azyr for Reforging and bring word of her betrayal. Not yet, at least.

Anvilgard was in Khainite hands. It was Morathi's greatest military triumph since the defence of Hagg Nar, and it opened a path to further conquests across the Realm of Fire. The city was renamed Har Kuron – 'City of Scales' in the Khainite tongue.

AS THE BLOOD FLOWS

The history of the Daughters of Khaine is one of constant strife and slaughter. Ever since Morathi first laid the foundations of Hagg Nar, the Brides of the Bloody-Handed God have spilled enough blood to drown entire continents. These proud warrior-zealots would have it no other way.

AGE OF MYTH

EXPANSION OF HAGG NAR

Led by Morathi, the Daughters of Khaine spread outwards from the temple-city of Hagg Nar. The High Oracle has stolen the secret of Malerion's shadow-shifting magic, and those shadowpaths allow swift travel over the vast distances of Ulgu. Fighting all manner of foes across all Thirteen Dominions, the Daughters of Khaine secretly expand, establishing dozens of Khainite temples and new sects.

BLOOD STRIFE

The expansion out of Hagg Nar is not without growing pains, as each of the newly formed sects of Khaine seeks to dominate the others. Unchecked, natural rivalries descend into open battle. Morathi allows the civil war to run its bloody course and uses it to weed out the weakest, as well as those she deems too ambitious.

A POWER TO RIVAL HAGG NAR

The temple of Ironshard – which will become home to the major sect of Khelt Nar – is founded by Morathi atop the mountain known as the Rothtor, which lies at the centre of a powerful spiral of shadow magic. To clear the surrounding lands, the shrine's Daughters of Khaine are forced to hunt down and kill hundreds of the most monstrous creatures of the Shadowlands, as well as dozens of Bonesplitter tribes. It is a task they revel in and which sees Khelt Nar develop rapidly.

FRAGMENTED GOD

Although she secretly knows that she possesses the only surviving shard of Khaine, Morathi commands the god's followers to hasten his return to full strength by finding more lost splinters, and so many war covens are dispatched on holy missions to scour the Mortal Realms.

AGE OF CHAOS

THE CATHTRAR DHULE

The treacherous valleys and gloom-forests of the Umbral Veil play host to a ferocious battle between the Daughters of Khaine and Slaaneshi trespassers. Countless aelves and daemon-worshippers meet an agonising end upon battlefields drenched in shadow and blood. The Khainites' greatest foe proves to be Luxcious the Keeper, a Greater Daemon who claims to be Slaanesh reborn. Her perfumed legions ravage great swathes of Ulgu, laying waste to several prominent temples including Neff-Taal, Prax Nar and Traith-Kine.

THE FIRST CAILLICH COVEN

With Luxcious's assault nearing Hagg Nar, Morathi is forced to call the first Caillich Coven, summoning a tithe of warriors from every Khainite sect to her aid. At the Battle of Druchxar, the High Oracle engages the forces of the Keeper of Secrets with the largest army of Scáthborn ever seen, a combined host of slithering Melusai and flocks of Khinerai. The resulting conflict rages over many days, until finally Morathi drives Heartrender through Luxcious's chest, banishing the would-be god to the Realm of Chaos.

BLOOD FEUD

The High Oracle commands Hag Queen Tayrathi of the Kraith to retrieve the Crimson Scianlar, an accursed dagger said to have been tempered in the blood of Khaine himself. Tayrathi travels to the Caverns of Aoch deep beneath Invidia, where the powerful relic can be found, only to come across Exalted Deathbringer Ugtai of the Eight-blooded and his warband, who also seek the powerful prize. The sweltering jungle caverns echo to the clash of axes and the bone-chilling cries of Sisters of Slaughter. Many of Tayrathi's Witch Aelves are hacked apart, but ultimately the Hag Queen triumphs; she draws the Crimson Scianlar from the pool of boiling blood in which it lies and with it slices open Ugtai's throat. Tayrathi's success earns her the cautious regard of the High Oracle.

AGE OF SIGMAR

UNEXPECTED ALLIES

Sigmar launches his new war against the Dark Gods, sending forth great hosts of gleaming-armoured Stormcast Eternals. They make landfall first in Aqshy, but several detachments are also sent to search for Morathi in Ulgu. Concealing Hagg Nar behind illusory shadow-spells, the High Oracle observes the tactics of the strange, masked champions as they hew their way through several Chaos hosts. At last, she reveals herself and her armies at the Battle of Dolmen Heights, just as the Celestial Warbringers sent to find her are assailed by a shrieking cavalcade of Slaaneshi Hedonites. In the aftermath of the engagement, an alliance of convenience is arranged between Azyr and Hagg Nar.

FUNGAL LUNATICS

Seeking to spread the filth of the clammydank across the Umbral Veil, an infestation of Gloomspite Gitz led by the legendarily repugnant Madcap Shaman Nitbug Dribblesnot surges out of the Inkspoil Mines. This green tide swarms across the darksome valleys of Va-Leth, leaving forests of poison-spewing mushrooms in its wake. Cackling away on a red-spotted fungal throne at the heart of his squelchy and mildew-ridden kingdom, Dribblesnot takes to calling himself the new 'Loonking'. His ambitions are shattered by a war coven from Khailebron, who utilise cunning illusions to slip past hordes of Moonclan Grots and into the Shaman's war camp. After a brief but ferocious skirmish with Dribblesnot's cadre of rabid Fanatics, the Khainites nail the crystallised form of the would-be Loonking to his own fungal shrine, frozen forever in the grip of unimaginable agony.

THE CULT EXPANDS

Over the centuries following the Realmgate Wars, Cities of Sigmar are erected across the Mortal Realms. Morathi is swift to install elements of the Khainite cult in these nascent strongholds, sensing a chance to spread her eyes and ears across the lands. With the God-King's grudging acquiescence, shrines and fighting pits erected in honour of the Bloody-Handed God can soon be found in several major free cities.

DEATHSTORM OF SHYISH

Nagash's grand plans come to terrible fruition, and a great tidal wave of undeath is unleashed across the realms. The spirits of the dead rise up across Ulgu.

TEN THOUSAND CUTS

It is said that not even the mightiest blow can slay Gruntlefist the Great. Yet when a war coven from Khelt Nar is sent to curtail one of the Mega-Gargant's violent rampages, they test the truth of that by striking not once, but ten thousand times. With every well-placed Khinerai javelin and arcing slice of a Witch Aelf's blade, Gruntlefist loses a trickle of blood, and mind-fugging magics dull his already lacking wits. The brute's waxy hide is soon covered with a lattice of shallow cuts. Many aelves are squashed flat by the Mega-Gargant's flailing feet, but eventually, Gruntlefist's mighty swipes begin to slow and his legs start wobbling beneath him. Exhausted, he topples to the earth, flattening a small forest in the process. The bloodthirsty Khainites proceed to flay Gruntlefist alive, capturing gushing torrents of gargant blood.

ASCENSION

Morathi ascends to godhood in a great ritual at Hagg Nar. She announces herself as Morathi-Khaine, the reincarnation of the Bloody-Handed God. The divinity she has desired for so long is now hers – but not without cost: her essence is split into two distinct forms joined by a single, fractured consciousness. Unbeknownst to the newborn goddess, her ritual allows something terrible to slide into reality – a protean essence bearing the mark of her ancient nemesis, Slaanesh.

HAR KURON RISES

Exulting in her new-found power, Morathi desires to expand the reach of Hagg Nar beyond Ulgu. To that end, she provokes an insurrection in the Aqshian port-city of Anvilgard. In the resultant confusion, the Daughters of Khaine seize the city, capturing its small garrison of Anvils of the Heldenhammer and putting its mortal armies to the sword. The souls of Anvilgard's many citizens are granted to the Idoneth in a symbolic gesture of unity. The city itself is renamed Har Kuron – 'City of Scales' in the Khainite tongue.

SHADOW PACT

Wishing to secure the outskirts of her newly annexed city, Morathi unites with the Idoneth of the Ionrach Enclave in order to seize the nearby strongholds of Fort Foothold and Gladium. The mists of the ethersea roll in, enveloping terrified Freeguild sentinels in a fug of confusion. Before they can react, screaming packs of Witch Aelves are in amongst them, slaughtering any who resist and offering up the rest as tribute to their Deepkin allies.

HEAVENS' WRATH

Lord-Veritant Keiser Ven Brecht – captured during the fall of Anvilgard – escapes through the intervention of an unknown benefactor and brings word of Morathi's betrayal to the God-King. Sigmar's fury is great. He dispatches three Warrior Chambers from the Hammers of Sigmar to retake the city. They find the armies of Khainite city Har Kuron ready and waiting, the Daughters of Khaine standing defiant alongside Dreadspears and armoured Drakespawn Knights. Battle is joined with terrible zeal. Storm-forged hammers descend with crushing force, while Witch Aelves stab and slice at gorgets and eye sockets as they shriek their blood-chilling prayers to Khaine. For all the ferocity of the Har Kuronites, they are outmatched and driven back to the very gates of the conquered city.

It is then that cloying mists sweep in from the Searing Sea, bringing with them great hosts of Namarti Thralls and eel-riding Akhelian warriors to surround the Stormcast Eternals. At that moment, Morathi-Khaine and her elite Vyperic Guard appear upon the battlefield. The Shadow Queen descends from on high in a flashing blur of scales, smashing dozens of shield-bearing Liberators to the ground. Suddenly, it is the Stormcasts who find themselves on the verge of disaster. At that pivotal moment, the skies split apart, and a coruscating column of lightning carries the Celestant-Prime to earth. In a voice that thunders over the clash of battle, the God-King's champion orders a halt to the killing. To the surprise of all, save perhaps Morathi herself, he offers a parley. The goddess accepts.

A BREAK IN THE STORM

Morathi-Khaine and the First-Forged Angel meet at Dauntless Hall, formerly the centre of governance in Anvilgard, which Morathi has converted into a luxurious place of residence. They speak alone for more than a day, and not even the goddess's most trusted agents are privy to their words. When the summit is over, the Celestant-Prime emerges and orders the Hammers of Sigmar to withdraw from the city. Har Kuron is to remain in the hands of Morathi – for now, at least. What has been promised in return, Morathi does not say.

DOMINION OF SHADRAC

In the wake of her successful seizure of varanite, Morathi returned swiftly to Hagg Nar, her fortress stronghold in the Shadrac Convergence. There she oversaw the beginning of a grand ritual, while her armies prepared to repel any opposing army that might dare to interrupt the High Oracle's holy work.

DOMAIN OF MORATHI

Hagg Nar is the pre-eminent power in the region known as the Shadrac Convergence, where eight of Ulgu's Thirteen Dominions meet amidst a tangle of jagged coastlines and narrow, treacherous seas. The temple-city sits atop a font of shadow magic known as the Helleflux that constantly spews thick mists. It is this arcane nexus that makes the Umbral Veil perhaps the darkest region of the Shadowlands, ever smothered by a pall of blackness.

LOOMING THREATS

Though Morathi's influence stretches far across Shadrac, her control is by no means absolute. The free city of Misthåvn is a growing power, its impressive navy already far larger than the smaller, elite fleets of Hagg Nar. The Idoneth Deepkin are also a constant threat, for the depths of the shadowsea provide the perfect cover for their raiding parties.

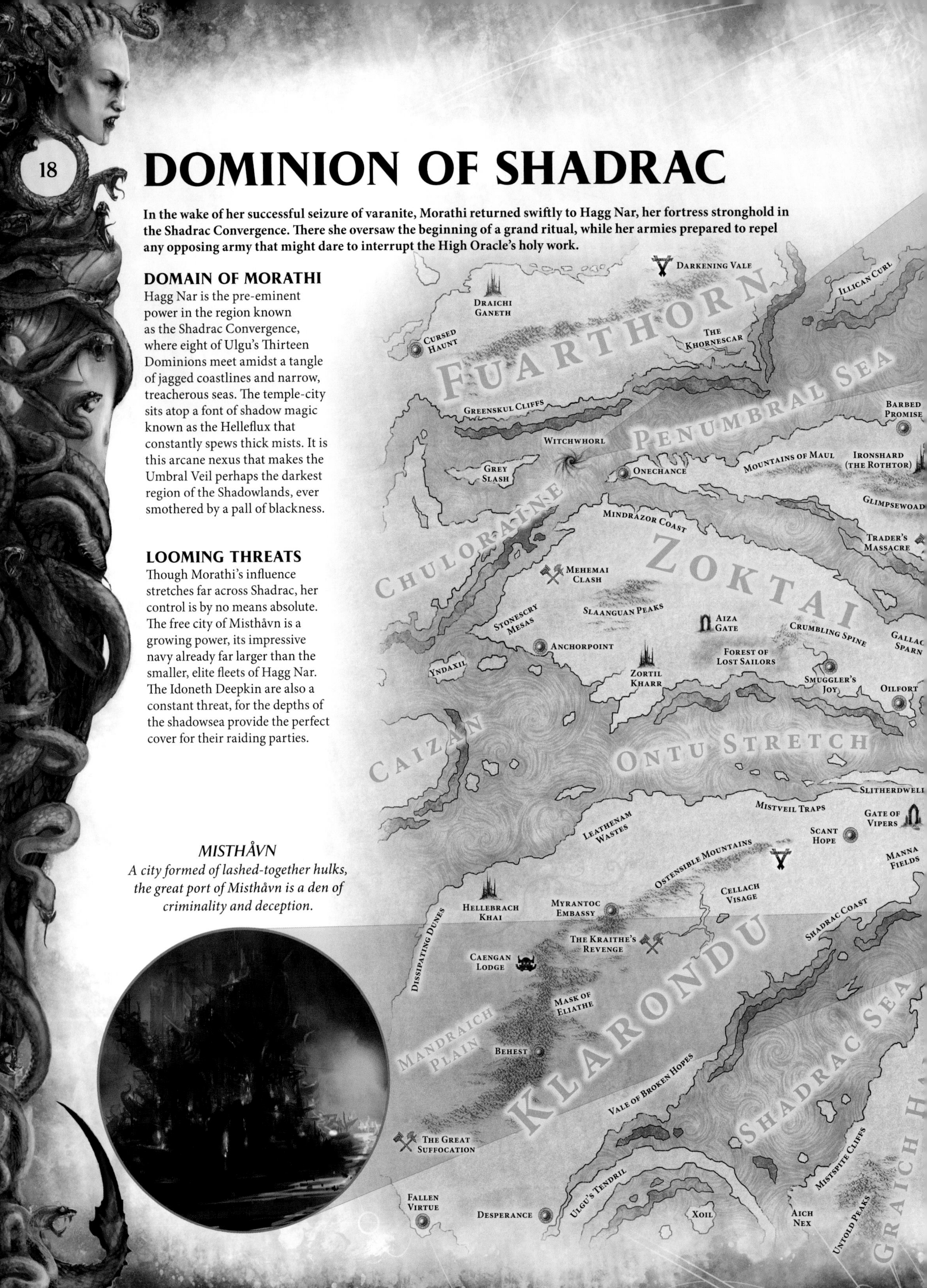

MISTHÅVN

A city formed of lashed-together hulks, the great port of Misthåvn is a den of criminality and deception.

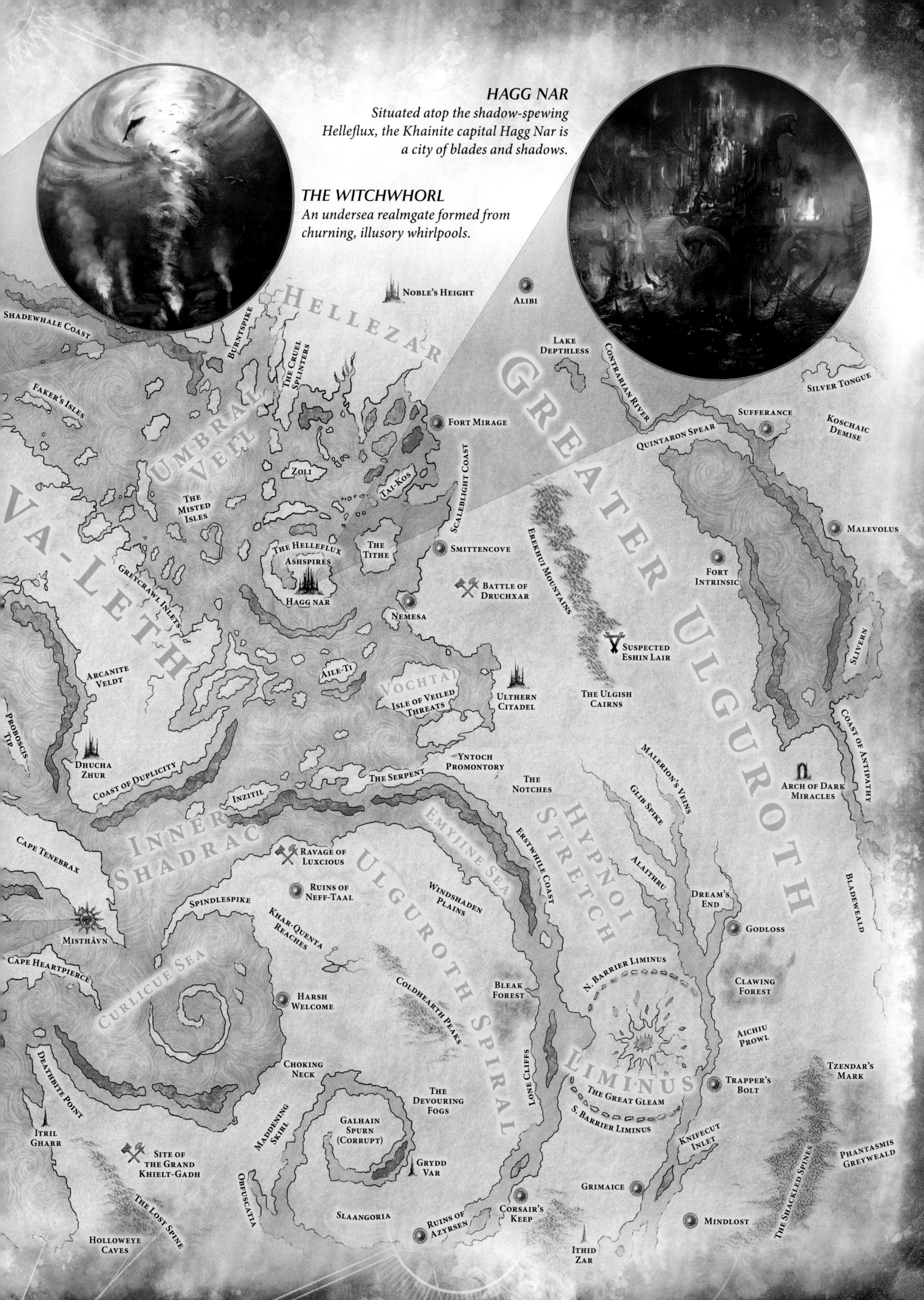

HAGG NAR

Situated atop the shadow-spewing Helleflux, the Khainite capital Hagg Nar is a city of blades and shadows.

THE WITCHWHORL

An undersea realmgate formed from churning, illusory whirlpools.

CITY OF THE FIRST TEMPLE

Ulgu, the Realm of Shadow, is a place permeated by lies and illusion. The temple-city of Hagg Nar, heart of the Khainite empire, can be found here, built atop a jagged island at the centre of the Umbral Veil. From this seat of power, the goddess Morathi plots expansion and conquest.

Hagg Nar is a dark and formidable metropolis, a shrouded place of reaching spires and darksome streets that rings not to the vibrant sound of commerce but to the clash of blades and the screams of sacrificial victims. What was once a lonely shrine to a long-absent god has transformed into a thriving centre of power, a city-state to rival any of the great Cities of Sigmar.

At its centre is the Helleheart, the great temple in which Morathi holds court. Here, the goddess and her High Priestesses direct the faith, issuing commands and decrees that will spread the influence of the Khainite cult across the realms. Helleheart is a vast and imposing structure that stretches from the skies to the deep caverns, a bladed fortress filled with sacrificial chambers, gladiatorial pits and other, darker places forbidden to all but the goddess and her retainers.

Hagg Nar is connected to the shadowpaths of Ulgu by many secret portals, each guarded by contingents of elite Scáthborn.

None but Morathi know how many Melusai dwell within the great brood-caverns of Slithásarath deep beneath her capitol.

Of the many gladiatorial pits in which the Daughters offer worship to Khaine through blood and death, few rival Kynith Cáillir, a many-tiered arena that is the pride of Hagg Nar.

In an attempt to consolidate her power, Morathi is gradually replacing the old depictions of Khaine with awe-inspiring iconography representing herself. In time, the faith shall be reshaped in her own image, and few will even remember the true origins of the Khainite cult.

THE WAR COVENS

War covens are the most important organisations to the Daughters of Khaine, for it is through violence that the Khainites expand their territories, defend their temples and worship their god. The structure and hierarchy of war covens have been passed down from Morathi herself.

There are many sects of Daughters of Khaine, each worshipping a different aspect of the aelven god of battle and bloodshed. Although their rites and rituals might differ, all Khainites follow a strict hierarchy in their organisation: either they are warriors who serve in their religious order, or they are leathanam, disregarded menials who are little more than worker drones. All sects save the Kraith are composed of both.

When battle is called, a Khainite sect will send forth its warrior congregation known as a war coven. Larger sects – such as Hagg Nar or Draichi Ganeth – have hundreds of war covens across dozens of temples, while the smallest of sects might have but one of each. The leaders of a war coven also preside over their unique blood rites and rituals. However, first and foremost of them all, regardless of sect, is Morathi-Khaine. Her word is law for all Khainites, and she speaks with the iron voice of a true goddess.

Beneath Morathi are the High Priestesses, the majority of them Slaughter Queens and Hag Queens. These powerful figures are the keepers of each shrine's most sacred artefacts and the commanders of the Sisterhood of Blood. The true degree of authority held by these Daughters of Khaine varies between the sects, as do their specific titles. For instance, the Kraith rank Slaughter Queens above the others and refer to the leader of a war coven as a Bloodqueen, whereas Bloodwrack Medusae carry greater favour in Hagg Nar, and when one is appointed as leader of a war coven, she becomes a Saim-Supremas.

Nevertheless, Morathi can alter any ranking with but a word. Should she favour a particular Kraith Hag Queen over a Slaughter Queen, the war coven's leadership will shift accordingly. Morathi has always been a canny strategist, unbeholden to tradition or cumbersome notions of fair play. Should the need arise, she will alert her extensive network of utterly loyal spies, murderers and assassins. Collectively known as the Shademarked, these include the deadly Khainite Shadowstalkers.

The troops of a war coven are divided into two categories: the Sisterhood of Blood and the Scáthborn. Covenite warriors from the Sisterhood of Blood are the most commonly seen, and to many, they are the face of the Daughters of Khaine. They are the Witch Aelves and Sisters of Slaughter, the gladiatrices who take part in public ritualised combat and shady pit fights. While such bouts develop the participants' fighting prowess and offer them the potential to move upwards in the hierarchy, all members of the Sisterhood of Blood long for the rapture of war, where they might be granted Khaine's divine blessings.

The Scáthborn, also known as the Trueborn, Shadowborn or Morathi's Handmaidens, are those creatures formed from the aelf-souls regurgitated by Slaanesh and reformed by Morathi. They are the Melusai and the Khinerai, beings whose new and twisted forms are often kept out of sight of outsiders, whether hidden away in darkened shrines or veiled by illusion. However, ever since Morathi claimed the power of a goddess, they have been sighted in ever greater numbers, fighting at the head of her conquering armies. These expeditions are typically led by feared Scáthborn generals such as the Melusai Ironscales – warlords created for the sole purpose of obliterating the enemies of Hagg Nar.

Most sects treat the Scáthborn as elite warriors; they hold a higher individual and unit ranking than their more comely kin from the Sisterhood of Blood. Certainly, Morathi uses them exclusively for her own honour guard – the vaunted Vyperic Guard – as well as her elite aerial attack formations. The exception is the Kraith; these Khainites are wanderers with no dedicated temples of their own, and as such they have fewer opportunities to conceal the Scáthborn. They do count them amongst their number, hidden by illusion, but they tend to rank them less highly than other sects.

The strict hierarchy employed by the Khainites is essential. The Daughters of Khaine are supreme warriors, but their fervour and bloodlust must be directed carefully to maximise its murderous power. The strengths of the covens lie in their mastery of the sudden ambush and the sheer speed and ferocity of their attacks. They are a blade that, when well-aimed, can sink into the vital organs of any foe.

'Hear me, my sisters, and I will tell you the one truth that matters: power. It matters not where or how we acquire it, only that we do so. We have all felt the taint of what happens to those who are defeated, and it must never happen again. Rise, my Scáthborn, for you are my will...'

- Morathi addressing her Melusai

THE IRON HEART OF KHAINE

Morathi was certain that Khaine had been destroyed when her blood rituals in his name no longer rejuvenated her and she was forced to use shadow magic to extend her life. History had also taught her that the aelven gods were cyclic beings, and that if any part of them remained, they might one day rise again. Even while construction of the temple of Hagg Nar was underway, she discovered echoes of the lost god. In the memory of Khaine, she saw a glimmer of potential, and a plan began to take form in her scheming mind. Alas, her searches – both physical and mystic – uncovered no trace of the Murder God, until finally she heard the faintest of heartbeats in her dreams.

Guided by prescience, Morathi began a quest that would take all her guile and arcane skill, but eventually she found what she sought – Khaine's Iron Heart. It lay intact and was once again beginning to throb with resurgent power. The treasure was guarded by Kharybtar, Father of Kharibdysses. Sensing that the godbeast would be resistant to hostile sorcery, Morathi resorted to trickery and illusion, as she was desperate to claim the Iron Heart before it drew the notice of others – most especially her son, Malerion.

Yet when attempting to wrest the object for her own, she angered Kharybtar and was forced to do battle. It was an epic struggle that lasted for thirteen days, until Morathi, in her true form, constricted the godbeast in her crushing coils. However, before losing consciousness, Kharybtar dealt her a dire blow. Only her ability to absorb the energies beginning to pulse from her new-found treasure allowed Morathi to survive and return with her secret to Hagg Nar.

What happened to Kharybtar none can say. It is rumoured that the wrathful godbeast still follows the scent of Morathi and that he will one day hunt her down. If this is true, that battle will be one to shake the realms to their core. With regard to the Iron Heart itself, Morathi keeps it close to hand, weaving complex illusions to conceal the truth as to which of her two vastly different physical forms possesses the powerful artefact.

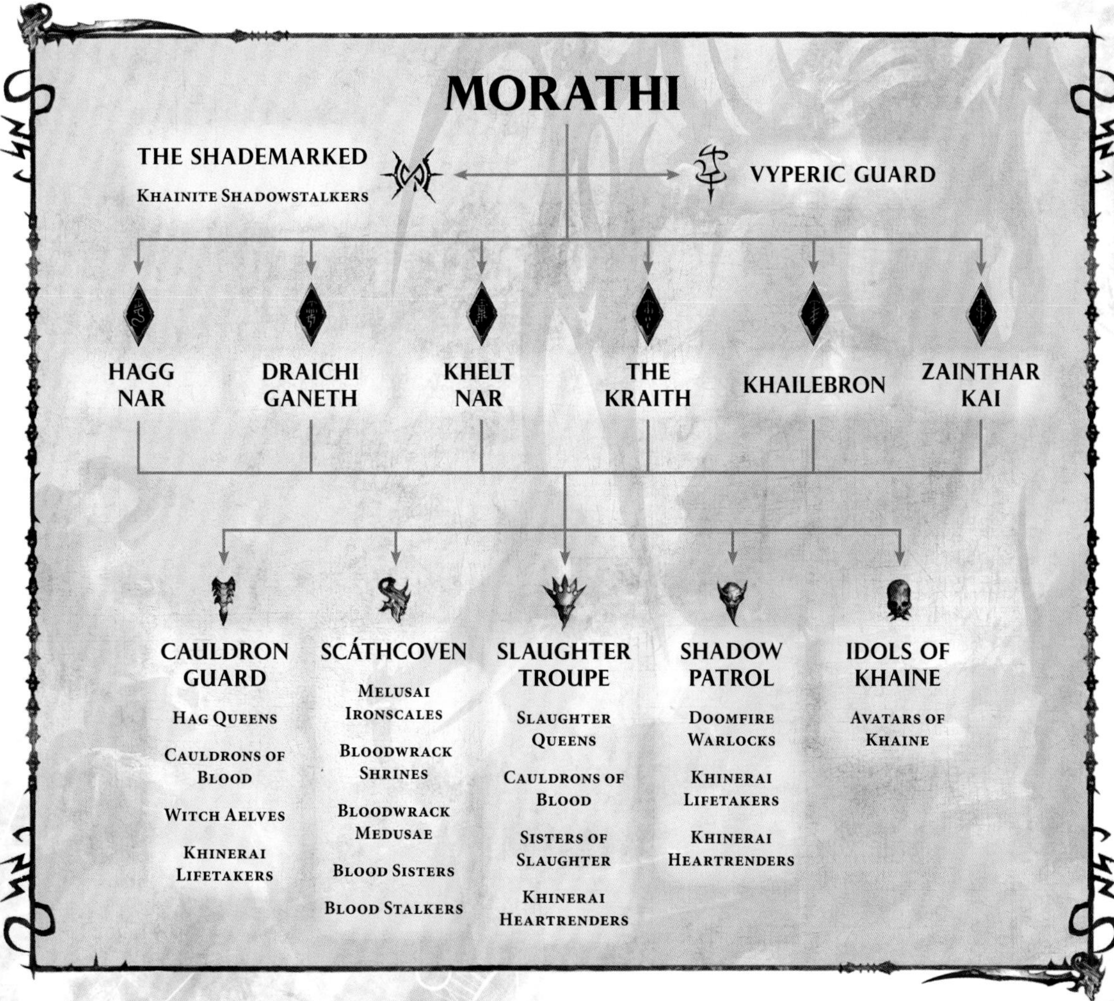

HAGG NAR

First and grandest of the Khainite strongholds, Hagg Nar has, over the centuries, grown into a powerful city-state. The Daughters of the First Temple regard themselves as the most pious of all Khaine's worshippers, and their mastery of blood rites and gruesome incantations is second to none.

Hagg Nar is where Morathi first established herself in Ulgu, where she rediscovered her faith and pledged herself anew to Khaine. This sacred legacy inspires the warriors of the First Temple to commit increasingly gruesome acts of violence in their leader's name.

Hagg Nar lies deep in the Umbral Veil, the darkest region of the Shadowlands, atop a mountainous island constantly lashed by the pitch-black waves of the Penumbral Sea. It was constructed atop the Helleflux, a geyser of shadow magic that spews shrouding mists. The greatest icons of the Khainite cult are here, including the Svartlepit and the Mother Cauldron, the Máthcoir. Hagg Nar remains the capital for all Khainite sects, a place where any aelf dedicated to the Murder God must one day pilgrimage. The sect also maintains control over several lesser strongholds in Ulgu as well as smaller shrines in many of the Cities of Sigmar.

It is said by other, jealous sects that the coven sisters of Hagg Nar receive the greater portion of Morathi's blessings; in many ways, this accusation appears to hold some truth. Few could credibly argue that this honour is not deserved, however.

Hagg Nar has always been at the forefront of Morathi's endless and brutal war against Chaos. During the Cathtrar Dhule, it was the Daughters of the First Temple who bled in defence of their home city, repelling countless daemonic invasions at the cost of untold lives. It was they, too, who led the fightback against the Slaaneshi tides spilling into Ulgu, driving their kin into a murderous frenzy with the power of their bloodthirsty liturgies. Their hatred of Chaos has not dimmed since.

When it comes to the blood rites, those rituals taught to all Daughters of Khaine by Morathi herself, instilling in them the terrible strength of their war-hungry deity, none can equal the mastery displayed by those of Hagg Nar. It is said that they possess secret knowledge of the incantations that will best court Khaine's favour. The Daughters of the First Temple are not shy in extolling their superiority over the other great sects, which does little to endear them to their kin. Still, their rivals would do well to avoid raising their ire, for Hagg Nar's armies are vaster and more powerful than those of any other sect.

Always ready to convert freshly drained blood into tribute, there are no war covens more likely to march with a Cauldron of Blood than those of Hagg Nar. Atop these rolling war-shrines are foreboding iron statues of Khaine; priestesses of the First Temple have mastered the art of bringing these metal giants to life through gory ritual. They are commonly sighted striding into battle alongside Hagg Nar's armies, hewing through enemy ranks or spewing torrents of boiling blood that melt through metal and flesh with ease.

DRAICHI GANETH

Martial-minded and scornful of those who skulk in the shadows, the Khainites of Draichi Ganeth seek to honour the Murder God through the perfection of the killing blow. They are gladiators beyond compare, never more comfortable than when they are carving their way through a worthy foe, faces smeared with freshly spilled gore.

Draichi Ganeth translates as 'the bladed killers'. Their main temple is found in the northern barrens of Fuarthorn in Ulgu, but their war pilgrimages and lesser shrines can be found across the realms. Indeed, aelves of this sect are amongst the most commonly seen of all the Daughters of Khaine, for while Hagg Nar has the greater numbers, its armies are more inclined to remain in the Umbral Veil, at the heart of the Khainite empire. Those of Draichi Ganeth, by contrast, are keen to explore new lands and seek out exotic new foes to kill.

There are few in the Cities of Sigmar who have not witnessed the ritual combat displays of Draichi Ganeth gladiators as they seek perfection of their gruesome art. In Hammerhal-Aqsha, the name of Mhaegra the Hag is whispered in fearful awe by all who have watched her deadly dance, while it is said that Vindicarum's Mother of Lashes has never suffered so much as a single cut in over a thousand bloody arena battles.

As they believe that it is through the killing blow – the act of beheading in particular – that Khaine is most honoured, Draichi Ganeth has earned the epithet 'the Executioner's Cult'. Its faithful members are not too proud to hire themselves out as mercenaries, as long as they consider the allotted quarry worthy of their time.

Those of Draichi Ganeth abstain from the use of poisons and regard the more shadowy Daughters of Khaine as beneath them, for they staunchly believe that a true warrior has no need of anything but athletic poise and prowess with a blade. In particular, Draichi Ganeth has a long and bloody rivalry with the secretive Khailebron, who have no such compunction when it comes to matters of murder. Even Morathi has found it difficult to keep this mutual hatred in check. Dealings between the two sects often devolve into a mire of insults, threats and gruesome slayings.

The slaughter-cultists of the Kraith are considered worthy of slightly more respect, though their unrefined ferocity is still deemed to be gauche. On the rare occasion that one of the Crimson Cult's wandering covens makes its way to Fuarthorn, the two rivals will stage Yaith'ril – a sacred gladiatorial contest fought by the most renowned warriors from each sect. The loser must offer a punishing tithe of blood sacrifices and suffer an ignominious loss of face.

As befitting their bold nature, the warriors of Draichi Ganeth shun stealth and make no attempt to conceal their kills. Indeed, before battle, their war covens often herald their approach to the enemy with gruesome triumphal processions in which prisoners are messily put to death. Draichi Ganeth typically fields a greater number of Witch Aelves than any other sect, a tide of blades that slices through the foe in a spray of viscera.

THE KRAITH

No other sect is as dedicated to slaughter as the Kraith, the dreaded Crimson Cult. The Kraith do not have their own temples or shrines, as they believe the true temple of Khaine is the battlefield. Instead, Kraith war covens wander the Mortal Realms in an endless pilgrimage in the name of the Murder God, offering their services to anyone who needs something killed – preferably in the most gruesome manner possible. They possess none of the militaristic restraint of the Draichi Ganeth, and their 'bloodless rituals' never remain so for long.

Those dedicated to the Kraith sect sneer at the Executioner's Cult, finding their controlled moderation to be weakness in another guise; it is their belief that the Daughters of Khaine were meant to bathe in blood not daub it on daintily. A kill need not be artistic or honourable; it is the killing itself that matters. The most famous of the Kraith is Krylla, a Slaughter Queen feared by foes and allies alike. It was she who perfected the art of coating blades with the deadly venom of Nagendra, a rite many Hag and Slaughter Queens have adopted.

Crimson or burgundy garments are the visual hallmarks of the Kraith. Their metal accoutrements usually have a red-gold trim, which contrasts with the cold green sheen of their armaments.

KHAILEBRON

The ways of the Khailebron are secretive, which is fitting, as they are a sect that worships Khaine's aspect as the assassin or unseen killer. There is but one temple dedicated to their cause, and its location is itself a carefully guarded secret, known only to those already sworn to their clandestine creed. By and large, the Khailebron are a nomadic sect that travels between the temples of the other sects. They act as a troupe of blade dancers, but in reality, they are on secret missions assigned to them by Morathi. Should allies or even rebellious factions of Khainites cause Morathi any problems, she will turn to the Khailebron.

The Great Sorceress herself has taught the Khailebron shadow magics, and their war covens march under the cover of thick, cloying clouds of mist. No matter what the foe sees, or thinks they see, the Khailebron still manage to emerge from unexpected quarters, striking quickly and with great surprise, often mortally wounding their prey before they can even raise their blades.

Blending in with the shadows, the leather and cloth worn by the Khailebron is dyed dark blue or purple. Their armour is brass or bronze, dulled to minimise any telltale glint, and their skin is often tattooed with jagged black designs.

KHELT NAR

Khelt Nar is the fastest growing of the sects established by Morathi. Its rise began with the construction of the Ironshard, a single Khainite shrine founded by the High Oracle atop a flat-topped mountain of iron known as the Rothtor. Seeing the potential in that bounteous natural resource, Morathi used powerful sorcery to mould an imposing stronghold from the enormous ferrous precipice and the lands surrounding it. Despite the layers of shadow magic that obscure the temple-fortress of Khelt Nar, the forces of the Ruinous Powers have located and invaded it no fewer than six times. Each attack has thus far been thwarted, but it has meant that the war covens of Khelt Nar have developed a hatred of Chaos that far transcends even that of their rival sects.

Utilising the veins of precious umbral metal that run throughout the Rothtor, they have also perfected the art of crafting masterful weapons, most notably kuirath – blades infused with an obfuscating curse. Those struck by such a blade find their minds engulfed by darkness and confusion as potent shadow-stuff spills into their veins. Dazed and reeling, these unfortunates prove easy prey for the Khainites' superior knife-work. The secret of crafting kuirath is fiercely guarded by the sect, for its rivals would dearly love to claim such knowledge as their own.

ZAINTHAR KAI

The Mortal Realms have only recently been exposed to the wrath of the Zainthar Kai – the Blood Saints, the first and most revered of the Scáthborn. For centuries, Morathi kept the existence of this sect a secret to all but her most trusted allies; she deployed them only in battles of the utmost import, most commonly in the deadliest engagements of the Cathtrar Dhule. Their brood nests and roosts lay deep underground, hidden behind webs of illusion, awaiting the moment of their mistress's ascension. Only now that Morathi-Khaine has claimed the power of a goddess and thrown off the shackles of mortality does she openly parade her finest Melusai warriors, each of whom proudly has the boiling blood of Khaine flowing through her veins.

Seen as holy beings by their kin, the Zainthar Kai cut a fearsome sight: crimson tears spill from their eyes, and their scales and leathery wings are flushed with sacred blood. Fearless and assured of their superiority over lesser beings, Scáthborn of this sect do not flee from battle, for to do so would dishonour their divine legacy. The greatest Zainthar Kai broodcrones blaze with the power of Khaine. Their cursed blood is so richly potent with his rage and passion that those nearby are stricken with agony, boiling gore pouring from their orifices in a hissing tide.

MORATHI

Finally, Morathi has attained that which she sought above all else – the power of divinity. Yet ascension has not come without cost. The nascent goddess has been divided into two physical forms that share a single consciousness: the regal sorceress Morathi-Khaine and the wrathful monstrosity known as the Shadow Queen.

Throughout her impossibly long life, Morathi has walked many paths and mastered countless disciplines. She is a cunning diplomat and a fearsome warrior, a devious ruler, a speaker to daemons and the mother of a tyrannical god. As fluid and changeable as the shadows of the realm she calls home, she has witnessed the death of a world and the fall of more kingdoms and petty empires than she can remember. Few beings in existence can claim a fraction of her skill in the magical arts – with little more than a flick of her hand, Morathi is able to summon formless horrors from the umbral realm to savage her foes or to blast them with bolts of icy darkness.

A manipulator and schemer without peer, Morathi has manoeuvred herself into position as one of the foremost powers in the realms. Through sheer cunning and boldness, she has claimed the near limitless might of a true goddess – a victory that has only strengthened the devotion of her zealous followers, the Daughters of Khaine. Morathi most often presents herself as a regal and stunningly beautiful aelf, framed by bladed wings of gleaming shadow-metal. In this guise, she goes by the name Morathi-Khaine, purporting to be the second coming of the Bloody-Handed God. Skilled in both murder and magic, Morathi-Khaine prefers to call upon the very shadows to rend and tear her foes apart, though she is not averse to more direct methods of attack – her ability to inspire a zealous frenzy in her followers is as lethal a weapon as her ensorcelled spear, the infamous Heartrender.

This queenly vision is the image Morathi wishes to present to the world, but when she is threatened or angered beyond reason, she calls forth a far darker aspect. Known as the Shadow Queen, this war form is a towering, serpentine monstrosity with enormous bat-like wings and a mane of venomous snakes. Though she lacks the magical might of Morathi-Khaine, the Shadow Queen more than compensates for this with the intensity of her bloodlust. Filled with monstrous power, she can pulverise stone walls with her lashing coils, and those who meet her dreadful gaze must possess a will of iron, lest their blood boil in their veins and they burst in a splatter of gore. She wields a shadow-simulacra of Heartrender, an oversized version of the legendary weapon that befits her formidable stature.

The wider world – including the majority of Hagg Nar's denizens – believes the Shadow Queen to be a monstrous ally of Morathi-Khaine's, perhaps some creature summoned from the darkest corners of the Shadowlands. This misconception serves the sorceress's purpose, but the truth is far stranger. One of the aelven king-souls devoured by Morathi during her ascension to godhood found the strength for a final act of vengeance before obliteration. They struck their assailant a fearsome psychic blow, cleaving her physical form in two and tearing at the foundations of her innermost self.

Morathi-Khaine and the Shadow Queen are one being, joined by the single soul that is Morathi. The former represents all her cunning and stately grace, while the Shadow Queen is an embodiment of her bottomless reserves of resentment and rage – a monstrous shadow that is no less emblematic of the goddess's true self. Taking to the battlefield together, these twin aspects form a terrifying union of martial and arcane might that is capable of obliterating entire armies.

Nevertheless, worrying questions regarding the nature of Morathi's apotheosis do linger. The goddess faces a constant battle to balance the two clashing aspects of her psyche. In times of great strife, the appeal of the Shadow Queen's straightforward, murderous hatred becomes very difficult to deny, and the composed power of Morathi-Khaine wavers. Some of the goddess's most loyal servants have heard her muttering and ranting alone in her chambers, although none would ever think of disclosing such disturbing matters – not least because Morathi would have them flayed alive. The ragged wound in Morathi's godly soul may never truly heal, and she wonders if the final cost of her ascension is yet to be revealed.

As for Khaine, what little essence remains of the dead god is contained within the Iron Heart: an artefact of unfathomable power now possessed by Morathi and exploited for her own ends. The Iron Heart pulses with divine power that repels assaults both physical and arcane in nature. This protection extends to both Morathi-Khaine and the Shadow Queen, for the shared soul of the goddess unites both of her physical forms. This is not always a boon – what afflicts one likewise affects the other, and so Morathi must ensure that the Shadow Queen's hateful malice does not lead both into terrible danger.

Although she wields the Iron Heart, Morathi carries none of Khaine's divine essence in her own veins. Despite the triumphant victory of her own ascension, it remains a delicate game that she plays. If her Khainite masses were to discover the true scale of her duplicity, they would surely seek the destruction of their usurper goddess. Yet such is Morathi's skill at manipulation, coupled with her ruthlessness in silencing dissenters, that her people remain ignorant of the scale of her deceit. For Morathi, the future is full of promise. At last, she wields the power to remake the realms in her own image and to take revenge on all who dared to doubt her.

QUEENS AND CAULDRONS

Hag Queens and Slaughter Queens are the High Priestesses of Khaine, and they lead the war covens both in battle and in blood rites. It is they, along with the ominous Cauldrons of Blood, who channel their deity's murderous energies, summoning them through swordplay and fierce invocation.

The High Priestesses of the Khainite cult are chosen from the covenite sisters – the Witch Aelves and the Sisters of Slaughter – by Morathi herself. Though she often selects the most zealous of the sect for such an honour, she has been known to nominate those who have earned her favour by other means. The initiation rites include a series of gory tests and blessings that culminate in the aspirant's immersion in a cauldron filled with shadow creatures from the nether-domains. Those who survive this final trial emerge more powerful than ever before, able to channel Khaine's violent spirit.

HAG QUEENS

The High Priestesses known as Hag Queens are the guardians of Khaine's mysteries and the leaders of their temple's rites. Through Morathi's teachings, the Hag Queens learn secret rituals, words of power and divine incantations that allow Khaine's energies to flow with all the gushing impetus of blood from a severed artery. It is the Hag Queens who mix any necessary poisons, and it is they who are responsible for the potion that drives their fellow Khainites into a rapturous battle-rage.

Known as witchbrew, this sacred concoction is derived from the blood of Slaughter Queens slain in the service of Khaine. Resonant with the fierce exultation that the deceased experienced in their final moments, this holy liquid is refined and blended through a sorcerous process known only to the High Priestesses. The resulting broth has the viscous consistency of clotting blood, and a single draught heightens the senses of the imbiber to supernatural levels, imbuing them with an uncontrollable bloodlust and robbing them of any sense of self-preservation. Their eyes rolling over white and their bloodstained teeth bared to resemble a nightmarish death mask, Khainites under the influence of witchbrew will ignore even the most horrific wounds as they slice and carve their foes apart.

Perhaps the most important duty of these priestesses is to prepare the Cauldrons of Blood for the rituals of rebirth. These rites keep the covenite sisters youthful in appearance and supple in body. All aelves, save the leathanam, have lifespans far greater than those whom they deem 'lesser races', such as men and orruks. Yet many of the covenite sisters, especially the Hag Queens themselves, have lived years beyond even the eldest of aelfkind. Without their regular rejuvenation baths, many would age rapidly or even die.

SLAUGHTER QUEENS

Those High Priestesses awarded the title of Slaughter Queen by Morathi are the martial leaders of the war covens, chosen for their skilled bladework and their fanaticism for dealing death. For a Slaughter Queen, the battlefield is her temple, and the jetting blood of an opened throat is her sacred offering to almighty Khaine.

In war, a Slaughter Queen fights with a sword in each hand, weaving a pattern of red ruination as she advances. The Blade of Khaine – blessed with the furore of war – strikes with blurring speed, while the Deathsword is imbued with Morathi's scorn, its enchanted edge slicing gaping clefts in flesh and armour with even the slightest stroke.

A Slaughter Queen wears little in the way of armour, instead relying upon feints, deft dodges and flawless acrobatics to avoid enemy blows. This High Priestess is a leader who can spur her war coven on to greater feats of violence or rally their wavering nerves through the sheer force of her will. No true Khainite can help but be inspired by the unrestrained butchery enacted by a Slaughter Queen. Where these priestesses roam, the land is soon watered with the hot blood of the freshly slain.

Though they prefer bladework to ministry, Slaughter Queens are still adept at channelling the hot rage of Khaine into devastating battle-prayers. All learn the killing words of power – appellations of Khaine that, when shouted at the correct pitch, can smite down an enemy or even blunt an incoming spell.

CAULDRONS OF BLOOD

For a battle worthy of their finest ritual offerings, the war covens of the Daughters of Khaine bring forth the greatest of their religion's icons – the Cauldrons of Blood. Mounted on iron-shod wheels, these mobile shrines grind forward, propelled solely by the incantations of their riders, as if the machine itself was lured onwards by the promise of carnage. Each Cauldron of Blood lies heavy with dark enchantments; its mere presence in the battleline motivates the Khainites.

When a Hag Queen accompanies the altar, she brings the blood within the iron vat to a furious boil until it gives off billowing clouds of crimson steam. This offers strange protections, and Khainites nearby find themselves able to shrug off wounds or dodge blows more easily. Those fortunate enough to be offered a draught of the cauldron's brew find themselves plunged into an ecstasy of violence, their martial prowess magnified by the Lord of Murder. Brought to life by blood rituals, the iron statue of Khaine upon the shrine roars its anger in torrents of molten metal blood or swings its massive sword to hack down those who dare close with the cauldron. Sometimes these iron golems are given a life of their own and stride across the battlefield autonomously, fighting alongside their worshippers as powerful icons of the Murder God.

It is said that the Cauldrons of Blood are gifts from Khaine himself, who bestowed them upon his Daughters as a reward for their dedication to his cause. This, at least, is Morathi's claim each time she gifts one of the great iron cauldrons to the grand temple of a newly founded Khainite sect. Created only in the underhall of Khruthú, at the heart of the First Temple, knowledge of the dark sorcery required to fashion these holy war-shrines belongs to Morathi and her most trusted servants alone. The Khainites see it as a sign of their god's favour that the cauldrons never seem to overflow, no matter how much blood is poured into them after battle – all assume Khaine himself takes the surplus as an offering.

This is not the case, however. Through Morathi's magics, those fluids flow back to Hagg Nar to the Mother Cauldron, the Máthcoir, whereupon Morathi absorbs and repurposes the blood's energies, using them for her own nefarious gain.

THE MOTHER CAULDRON

The immense iron cauldron known as the Máthcoir was created by Morathi to store the soul energies she had leached from Slaanesh. Within this vast receptacle, she blended raw shadow magic with her own blood in order to create new physical forms for these stolen souls. The Mother Cauldron also became the font through which the High Priestesses of Khaine channelled all their strange blood magic. It was, in essence, the source of Morathi's own power, constantly refilled by the sacrifices of her scattered war covens.

When she enacted her great ritual of ascension, Morathi filled the Máthcoir with pure varanite, channelling through it the spirits of thousands of slain Chaos worshippers. In doing so, she transformed the Mother Cauldron into a portal to the very gut of Slaanesh, through which she drew forth the powerful king-souls that, once consumed, would expand her power to that of a goddess. However, the Mother Cauldron was damaged – perhaps irreparably – by the ritual. Unable to contain the swelling energies summoned by Morathi, the iron surface of the Mother Cauldron splintered and cracked, and a flood of boiling varanite swept forth.

The extent of the damage to the Máthcoir remains unknown to all but Morathi and a handful of her closest agents. Nevertheless, whispers have spread throughout Hagg Nar that tell of the goddess's attempts to repair the splintered cauldron – attempts that have birthed a host of malformed monstrosities that shriek and hiss in the depths of Khruthú, where they are fed a regular supply of leathanam thralls…

WITCH AELVES

The heart and soul of the Daughters of Khaine are the warriors known as Witch Aelves. Bloodthirsty and eager zealots, they fight at the forefront of nearly every war coven, seeking to lose control in the wanton frenzy of battle to better honour their violent god.

Witch Aelves are devotees of Khaine, their entire lives dedicated to serving their bloodthirsty deity. In stoic fashion, they train endlessly. Though weapons practice and mock duels take up the majority of their daily lives, these are not mere military drills; they are religious ceremonies, treated with all the gravitas that other cults might use when reading their most holy of tomes or offering prayers to their god. For Witch Aelves, ritual combat hones martial prowess and sates a craving for violence, while duels fought against prisoners, captured beasts or gladiatorial opponents offer a chance to spill blood. However, it is only in battle where the followers of Khaine can truly immerse themselves in the holy rapture that bonds their souls with the Murder God.

Witch Aelves fight with long sacrificial knives known as sciansá – steel blades tempered in blood and blessed by the Hag Queens. The sciansá is a holy tool for the worship of Khaine. Its razor-sharp edge slices easily through flesh, while some bear a notch that, with a subtle twist, causes maximum pain and profuse bleeding. Whether wielded in a pair or accompanied by a bladed buckler, a Witch Aelf weaves her sciansá in a blurring flurry of deadly attacks.

Armour is generally considered an impediment to the art of slaughter, though Witch Aelves do wear enchanted bracers and pauldrons that can turn aside the rare blow that they fail to evade. There are very few Khainites that would willingly eschew the sensation of hot gore splattering across their bare flesh.

Before battle, it might be said that Witch Aelves are staid, reserved or even cold, but in the midst of combat, all of that is left behind. With an explosion of movement, Witch Aelves spin, feint, dodge and pirouette, twirling their blades in an increasingly violent dance. Steady voices become shrill with battlelust and chants become shrieks. The presence of High Priestesses of their order inspire them to greater acts of carnage still, as does their own vicious bloodletting.

As their battleline devolves from an ordered march into a whirlwind of stabbing and slicing, the Witch Aelves truly lose all self-control. Still-beating hearts are ripped from victims' chests and flesh is daubed with gore-red runes. Dancing like pale shadows, they weave a scarlet path through the orgy of destruction, revelling in the spray of jetting arteries. This exultant murder-trance can be terrifyingly unpredictable. There are many dark tales of Witch Aelves losing themselves utterly to the slaughter and turning their sacrificial knives upon supposed allies. These rumours have, of course, been vehemently denied by both Morathi and her High Priestesses.

SISTERS OF SLAUGHTER

Merciless masters of the lash, the Sisters of Slaughter leap into the fray and do not cease their flailing dance until all their foes lie dead. Sometimes, even that is not enough to stop these vicious killers; to them, mutilation and bloodshed are acts of purest devotion to their cruel deity.

To the Sisters of Slaughter, combat is everything. Their entire lives are dedicated to fighting – melee is worship, and only through mastery of it can they truly worship Khaine. They fight in an exaggerated style: spinning, leaping and posing dramatically as they use their whips and blades to trace ancient runes in enemy flesh.

The Sisters of Slaughter are a sub-cult considered extremist even by other Khainites. Whether absorbed by revenge or overcome with the murderous spirit of Khaine, the warriors take the vow of druharú and don masks of living metal. Once, these were worn solely for the Khielt-gadh, a ritual combat that recreated the mythic battles of Khaine against the Chaos powers. In an excruciating rite involving boiling blood and spells of bonding, those who would join the sisterhood permanently graft the helms onto their heads, the metal leering ever more cruelly as it scents blood.

Only the most committed choose the face of Khaine over beauty. The screaming lasts for hours. Yet the trial is not complete until they have fought a series of ceremonial duels against established members. Those who do not succumb to blood loss become Sisters of Slaughter – gladiatrices insanely dedicated to fighting in the name of Khaine.

Barbed whips known as kruip-lash are the weapon of choice for the Sisters of Slaughter, and each practises her weaponcraft to levels of skill and precision only an aelf could achieve. With a simple flick of her wrist, a Sister can crack her kruip-lash so that it shears a gloomfly in half – an amazing feat, for the thumbnail-sized insects blend in with the cloying mists in which they are found. When the barbed whips are used in battle, the effect is far more devastating: the serpentine coils snap out to sever limbs, lacerate eyes or puncture armour to flay the flesh beneath. Some Sisters battle with a short stabbing blade in addition to their lash, while others prefer a bladed buckler that can turn enemy strikes and deliver a lethal counter-blow of its own.

Dedicated as they are to unrestrained bloodletting, the fanatical armies of the Kraith are more likely to field vast numbers of Sisters of Slaughter than any other sect. The Crimson Cult holds those who wear the iron mask in great esteem. Indeed, the majority of the Kraith's Hag Queens and Slaughter Queens have ascended from the ranks of the sisterhood, having caught Morathi's eye through particularly extravagant acts of violence. Unsurprisingly, these High Priestesses are amongst the most ferocious figures in the Khainite cult, always seeking the deadliest battlefields upon which to offer bloody tribute to the Murder God.

BLOODWRACK SORCERESSES

Foes fall twisting in pain as the Bloodwrack Shrine closes upon them. Shadowy and disturbing images flash upon the arcane mirror, drawing opponents' eyes closer to the blood-bursting gaze of the writhing creature that slithers at its base. With a crash, the bladed shrine strikes home...

BLOODWRACK MEDUSAE

It is considered a high honour among Khainite aelves to be selected for the Slith-onóir. In this gory ritual, their flesh is pierced by the fangs of the hissing serpents that crown the Shadow Queen's skull. This results in the agonising transformation of the chosen into monstrous beings blessed with a portion of Morathi's strength and magic – the Bloodwrack Medusae.

Bloodwrack Medusae wield sorcerous energies, and their eyes blaze with the power of death. Any who meet a Medusa's gaze find their body exsanguinated in a welter of gore. Neither does the sorceress shy away from combat; wielding the razor-sharp gauntlet known as a whisperclaw in concert with a Bloodwrack spear, the Medusa can cut a swathe through any foes foolish enough to approach her.

Those selected for the Slith-onóir might be the rising champions of their sect, but some are chosen because they are openly contentious when it comes to Morathi's strictures. Regardless, after the ritual, Bloodwrack Medusae become Morathi's most faithful and loyal servants. Naturally resonant with arcane power, they eagerly absorb every scrap of the goddess's might, including malicious spells and curses of her own devising.

BLOODWRACK SHRINES

Some Bloodwrack Medusae are borne into battle atop mobile shrines. Propelled by unseen magics, the bladed Bloodwrack Shrine grinds forward to crash into the enemy battleline. Two shrineguards armed with long goadspears strike out, while the writhing Medusa uses her whisperclaw, Bloodwrack spear and deadly gaze to join the slaughter.

As formidable as the shrine is in close combat, it has another, more sinister purpose. A strange mirror known as a scáthmre stands at the shrine's centre, reflecting not just the Bloodwrack Medusa's deadly gaze but also an agonising aura, a shadowy projection of the scathing hatred harboured by the monstrous serpentine creature.

Such is the power of this dark emanation that it causes nearby foes to perish in the throes of unbearable torment. Eyes bulging, screaming at the top of their lungs, they writhe and lash in such a frenzy that they snap their own spines – much to the cruel enjoyment of the watching Medusa.

'Sssoon you too will feel your heart grow colder; you will shed your skin into scales and be reborn in the image of our one true master...'

- Final Ritual of the Slith-onóir

MELUSAI IRONSCALES

Cold hearts filled with the need for revenge, the Scáthborn war leaders known as Ironscales tear across the battlefield in a gory whirlwind. They cut their foes down with vicious blows from their serpent-headed staves before plucking out their crystallised hearts as an offering to the Bloody-Handed God.

The elite war leaders known as Melusai Ironscales are one of the most dangerous breeds of Scáthborn to slither from the depths of the Máthcoir. Even in the age of Morathi-Khaine, when the Scáthborn are no longer such a fiercely guarded secret, they are still a rare sight for most Daughters of Khaine; the Sisterhood of Blood believes that they are formed from souls whose faith in the Murder God allowed them to endure their torment. The truth is somewhat more complex.

The souls used in the creation of the Ironscales did indeed retain a sense of self better than most, but not because of zeal; rather, it was a burning desire for revenge against their race's age-old foe that allowed a wisp of self-awareness to cling on. Upon extracting these souls from Slaanesh, Morathi took special care in shaping and blending them with the dark secrets she had learnt, crafting a new generation of Scáthborn champions to serve in her devoted armies.

The Ironscales are Morathi's trusted inner coven and, as far as the lower-ranking Khainites are concerned, speak with the voice of the goddess. They are privy to truths concealed from most and are granted the honour of contributing to Morathi's increasingly regular councils of war, for even the goddess recognises their innate talent in military matters. Ironscales are responsible for the protection of Morathi-Khaine – such as she requires – and one of their number occupies a semi-permanent position as the commander of her elite Vyperic Guard, a retinue of hardened Scáthborn bodyguards.

As Morathi plots to seize ancient artefacts and sites of eldritch power to further her insidious schemes, it is the Ironscales who lead her conquering covens; the souls of these champions have been threaded with arcane wards that allow them to resist the magical energies they regularly encounter, though the ever-cautious Morathi has ensured that her own sorceries are not so easy to turn aside. There is no profit in unnecessary risk, after all.

Wielding curved sacrificial daggers and serpent-crested staves known as keldrisaíth, they loose bolts of shadowy energy into the foe and strike down their enemies with lightning-fast blows. The coiling serpents atop these weapons are more than simple decoration: when the correct words of power are spoken, they lunge forwards, distend their jaws and bury their sharp fangs deep into an enemy's chest, tearing out their heart in a single motion. By holding this gory offering aloft in supplication to Khaine, the Ironscales can tap into ancient blood sorcery, driving their Scáthborn kin into a violent frenzy that can collapse an entire battleline in a few gore-soaked minutes.

MELUSAI

The dreaded Melusai are Scáthborn who bear the lower bodies of great serpents. They are cruel, cold-blooded and eager to inflict pain – seemingly the ideal Khainites – and they serve Morathi as the elite ground-assault troops of her war covens.

The Melusai were once the souls of aelves devoured by Slaanesh. Upon being freed from that hellish incarceration, their energies were portioned off to Morathi. There, in the dungeons beneath Hagg Nar, these souls were mixed with shadow magic and Morathi's own blood to be reborn, reshaped in the image of their creator. The lower half of their body is that of a serpent, scaled and coiling with fierce strength, while the upper torso is indistinguishable from that of a female aelf.

Each of the Melusai is imbued with magic and the utmost faith in their mistress, along with a scornful hatred of their former enslaver, Slaanesh. They are allocated to each sect of the Daughters of Khaine, acting not only as elite guard formations but also as clandestine eyes and ears for Morathi, informing on those who question the order of things or ask too much about the new goddess's goals. Because of their strange appearance, Melusai were once confined to the shadows, either secreted inside the darkened temples of Khaine or disguised by illusion to appear as other aelves. Since her ascension, however, Morathi has been far more willing to send her finest warriors into battle for all to see. She claims that they are heralds of a new age – proof positive of her reincarnation as the Murder God. Now they slither forth at the head of her armies, a potent symbol of Khainite supremacy

Although it is rumoured that there might be additional forms, two kinds of Melusai are regularly seen amongst the war covens during open battle.

BLOOD SISTERS

Blood Sisters are powerful warriors employed either as bodyguards for High Priestesses or Bloodwrack Medusae or as a potent vanguard for the war covens. Each Blood Sister is equipped with a heartshard glaive – a heavy polearm ideal for driving through armour and ribs to impale an enemy's heart. Despite its size, the Melusai wield this weapon with prodigious grace, often carving their opponents apart before they can raise their own blades in defence.

Their fearsome kragath war-masks – crafted to recall Khaine's own terrible visage – are designed to inspire pure terror in the Blood Sisters' prey. Each kragath is also layered with illusory enchantments that allow the wearer to take the form of a normal aelf, should the occasion require it. Melusai sometimes walk amongst the ranks of the Khainite masses, gathering information for their mistress and keeping a predatory eye out for the slightest hint of discontent or blasphemy.

Blood Sisters can also channel the blackness of their tainted souls into a strike known as the scáth touch. The lightest contact from such a blow can transform the victim into an unmoving crystal statue that is still horrifically aware of its own metamorphosis. The undercrofts of Hagg Nar are filled with these living monuments, and the brood nests of the Melusai are likewise lined with unfortunate victims. Indeed, the walls of Morathi's own inner sanctum are carved from the crystallised corpses of hundreds of former rivals and enemies. Their horrified faces, twisted into expressions of indescribable agony, never fail to amuse the goddess.

As sensualists, the Blood Sisters consider an eternity of sensory deprivation the worst of all possible fates, hence their delight in inflicting it upon others. For a Blood Sister, the ultimate cruelty is to thrust her glaive quickly enough to slice out a foe's beating heart while transmuting them to still-living crystal. To be trapped forever in a state of unbearable pain is but a small sample of the torment the Melusai themselves have endured.

BLOOD STALKERS

The Blood Stalkers are Morathi's elite archers, a venomous guard who rain death from afar. Each bears a heartseeker bow, a weapon carved from the wood of the sentient ashdusk tree. The arrows loosed by such bows are blessed by Hag Queens and imbued with the same enchantments as those that guide Morathi's own spear, Heartrender. With uncanny accuracy, these missiles streak across the battlefield to pierce their targets' hearts.

In close combat, Blood Stalkers wield scianlar, long daggers forged to absorb the energies released when the bearer extracts the vital organs from the corpses of their victims after battle. Though they prefer to engage their prey at a distance, a Blood Stalker's ability with a blade should not be underestimated – they are Khainites after all, and all relish the sensation of thrusting a scianlar into soft, yielding flesh.

Though they are perfectly capable of speech, in battle, Melusai communicate via a series of graceful gestures and unspoken empathic signals. This allows Blood Stalkers to hunt their prey silently through the darksome valleys of Ulgu before launching a sudden and deadly ambush. The first their prey knows of the danger is when barbed missiles begin to rain down upon them.

Bands of Melusai typically hail from the same brood nest, further bonding them into a single, lethal weapon. The leader of a Blood Stalker pack is known as a Krone and is usually the eldest sister. Many employ the predatory creatures known as Blood Wyrms to track their quarry. Roughly the size of a hunting hawk, these winged serpents can sniff out a single drop of blood from a hundred leagues away. Their sharp, hooked fangs also eject an anticoagulant poison that causes blood to thin and flow like water, allowing the Blood Wyrm to bring down a target many times its size.

Of all the Khainite sects, it is the Khailebron who most revere their Blood Stalkers, seeing them as the perfect form of the unseen slayer. Disguised Melusai walk amongst the sect's nomadic troupes of blade dancers, camouflaged behind a shroud of illusion. A common form of sacrifice among the Khailebron is to release their most dangerous prisoners in Melusai territory, watching from afar as the Blood Stalkers track them down. Though these sacrifices are sometimes granted weapons and armour to make the contest more interesting, such pursuits only ever end one way – in the quarry's bloody, painful death.

Hag Queen Kóira smirked as the bloodied prisoner was deposited at her feet. The warriors of Draichi Ganeth who had claimed this prize bowed to their High Priestess.

'You have done well,' Kóira said, rising to her feet.

She drew her blade and slid it under the chin of the captive, raising the aelf's eyes to her own.

'Welcome, Sinethra,' said Kóira. 'It has been too long.'

Sinethra's piercing yellow orbs showed no hint of fear.

'You were warned, Kóira,' she hissed. 'By decree of Hagg Nar. Our feud was to end. Now I offer you one final mercy. Release me, and your death will at least be swift.'

The Hag Queen leant down to whisper into her rival's ear.

'My agents were very careful,' she said. 'No one will find your body, Sinethra. Your fate will remain a mystery.'

Sinethra smiled wide.

'Agony it is, then,' she said. 'I cannot say I am disappointed.'

A sudden lance of agony pierced Kóira's heart. She screamed and would have stumbled, were it not for the fact that her body was rooted to the spot. A terrible, crackling sensation rippled across her skin as it turned into black crystal.

Sinethra rose. Somehow she now carried a glaive, and atop its gleaming point Kóira could see her own beating heart.

The prisoner's rictus grin grew wider. It stretched hideously across her face, as flesh split apart and transformed into a burnished iron war-mask. At the same time, her lower torso contracted and twisted to become that of a great snake. Through her infinite agony, Kóira recognised the holy form of one of Morathi's most favoured Melusai.

'Foolish,' the Scáthborn said. 'To think that your treachery would escape the notice of a goddess.'

AGENTS OF SHADOW

Morathi does not solely rely upon the fierce battlelust of the Khainite faithful to achieve her aims. Her extensive and complex network of spies, assassins and other clandestine agents is almost unrivalled, stretching from deepest Ulgu to the gleaming palaces of Hammerhal.

DOOMFIRE WARLOCKS

The Doomfire Warlocks are the light cavalry of the war covens. They harass foes with blasts of arcane flame and volleys of black-fletched bolts, worrying the enemy's flanks and slaying unprotected targets. As the main Khainite formations are engaged, these swift riders charge in, scimitars drawn, to help overwhelm and finish off their distracted victims.

Up close, Doomfire Warlocks are gaunt and pallid, their black eyes haunted and lacking any emotion save spite. Emblazoned upon their brows are hateful runes that cause them great pain but are also vital in keeping them alive.

There are few male aelves in the cities of the Daughters of Khaine – fewer still in the military hierarchies of the war covens. This is by nefarious design. Only the weakest and most broken souls retrieved from Slaanesh are used to create male aelves, and these are destined to serve as leathanam, wretches exploited by the Khainites for menial labours and worse. They are worked hard, fed poorly and drained of blood in daily rituals. It is Khaine's wish that only the strong survive; the weak must either perish or perform some task deemed worthy enough to warrant the gift of maintaining their paltry existence.

Not all aelf males are formed from souls that have been recovered from their torturous existence inside the Great Enemy. Those birthed to covenite sisters in the conventional fashion are likewise afflicted with a weakness of the body and spirit. This too is no coincidence, for the High Oracle long ago wrought a secret malediction that would touch all sons born of the Daughters of Khaine, allowing her to siphon off a portion of their soul-stuff to add to the ever-growing font of power stored by the Máthcoir.

Despite the crippling odds stacked against them, some of these male whelps grow stronger than the others. These few, nurtured by the shadows themselves, develop an affinity with the darkness and an ability to absorb the mystical energies of Ulgu. Although Morathi recognises the potential of these males, she is leery of any power she herself has not granted. To ensure their faith, each is branded with runes of control – though they are told such marks are wards against the soul-thievery of Slaanesh.

KHAINITE SHADOWSTALKERS

Whenever Morathi desires a target discreetly slain or a potent artefact recovered from enemy hands, she sends forth her hand-picked agents – the Khainite Shadowstalkers. Only they are granted the honour of wearing the mircath, or shademark, a brand woven from Ulguan sorcery that grants extraordinary supernatural abilities yet leashes the bearer's soul eternally to Morathi's service. Able to leap from shadow to shadow and weave tools of murder from the very stuff of the night, these master assassins stalk and kill the many enemies of Khaine's chosen disciple.

Once marked for death, no quarry is safe from their blades. Shadowstalkers can transport themselves across unfathomable distances in an instant by slipping through the arcane pathways of the Umbral Web, an intricate pattern of shadow magic that connects each of the Eight Realms. Some even forge pacts with shadow daemons, so thoroughly mingling their blood with these half-corporeal monsters that, if cut, they bleed pure darkness. Using the foulest of sorceries, such beings can even command the shadow of a victim into murderous animation, directing it to strangle the life from its owner.

THE UMBRAL WEB

The Umbral Web is an extension of the fabled shadowpaths – a labyrinthine network that winds and wends its way between the realms. Formed by the darksome pall of Ulgu, this mysterious maze offers passage into lands unreachable by any other means. Distant locations across the Mortal Realms have been anchored to Ulgu by a series of shadowy waystones laid down by Morathi and her son, Malerion, during the Age of Myth.

Those who set foot inside the Umbral Web unprepared are never seen again. Not only are its shrouded depths almost impossible to navigate, there are terrible things that dwell in the shadows, among them smoke-winged nightmares that consider the mortal soul a particular delicacy.

Even worse, prolonged exposure to the Umbral Web causes the flesh and the soul to ebb away until, eventually, a traveller is transformed into a formless shade – a malicious entity of pure shadow.

Only Morathi and Malerion have discovered how to walk its gloom-shrouded paths, and even they cannot do so indefinitely. Thus, they employ disposable agents such as the Shadowstalkers to make use of the Umbral Web's potential, branding them with arcane runes that offer, at best, temporary protection. This also provides Morathi with a useful manner of disposing of those in her flock who display troubling signs of ambition.

KHINERAI HARPIES

Shrieking harridans of the skies, the Khinerai Harpies descend from the clouds upon membranous pinions. They are the winged Children of Morathi, her vengeance given flight, and nowhere on the battlefield is safe from their vicious, swooping attacks.

Similar to their kin, the Melusai, the Khinerai Harpies are the twisted offspring of daemon-tainted aelf-soul, Morathi's blood, dark magic and vengeance itself. All Khinerai are formed in Hagg Nar, where their broods can be found among the soaring peaks of the Ashspires. At each shade solstice, the ritual of Gristead takes place, and Morathi chooses flocks to dispatch to worthy Khainite sects across the Mortal Realms.

KHINERAI HEARTRENDERS

The Khinerai Heartrenders sweep out of the skies, dark streaks that cut swiftly through low clouds. With streams of vapour still clinging to their bodies, the winged aelves pull up, using their forward momentum to help launch cruelly barbed javelins with great force. These spike-ridden spears travel with such velocity that they can skewer both a mounted warrior and their steed and still maintain enough impetus to embed themselves deep into the ground. The Heartrenders do not stop to watch the gory aftermath of their arrival; always do they seek new prey, their powerful wings carrying them to another part of the battlefield in moments, javelins materialising out of the mists into their hands.

Constantly in motion, they quickly dart out of range of any return attacks, their hawk-sharp eyes scanning all the while for their next victim. Should a tempting enough target present itself, the Heartrenders will forego their missile assault and dive straight into combat – their barbed javelins are perfectly weighted for hand-to-hand fighting, and they can swiftly retreat back into the skies should the enemy bring overpowering numbers to bear.

KHINERAI LIFETAKERS

Tucking their wings close, the Khinerai known as Lifetakers plummet downwards at high speed. At the last moment, they spread their leathery pinions, halting their descent as they swing their sickle-blades with maximum force. Forged from priceless shadow-metal, these weapons are designed to slice open throats and remove heads with a single blow. Those foes who survive the Harpies' initial devastating assault can strike back, but any who fight the Khinerai must keep their wits about them, for these creatures are masters at using their claw-like heartpiercer shields not only to parry blows but also to puncture vital organs.

Even as nearby enemies rally to pin the Khinerai Lifetakers in combat, the Harpies rise above the melee in a flurry of beating wings, looking for the next vulnerable targets to strike.

Freed from the limitations of mortality, the new goddess Morathi seeks to drive all Slaanesh worshippers from her lands once and for all, a purge enacted by the terrifying Shadow Queen.

COVENS OF BLOOD

The Daughters of Khaine go to war in a terrifying procession, their razor-keen weapons and pale skin gleaming in the darkness as bubbling Cauldrons of Blood roll forward in their wake. To hear the ear-splitting cries of charging Witch Aelves and to see the zealous madness in their eyes is to know the certainty of one's bloody demise.

A Slaughter Queen leads her war coven in gruesome pre-battle rites, stirring Khaine's faithful into a murderous, zealous frenzy that will ensure that the bloodthirsty god's desire for carnage is sated.

Morathi-Khaine

The Shadow Queen

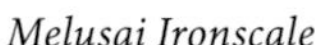

Melusai Ironscale

A Melusai Ironscale and her retinue seek to clear an infestation of squig-riding grots from their sacred grounds, puncturing the hides of the creatures' swollen mounts with graceful strikes of their war glaives.

Hagg Nar Blood Stalker

Hagg Nar Krone

Hagg Nar Blood Stalker

Hagg Nar Blood Sister

Hagg Nar Gorgai

Zainthar Kai Blood Sister

Cauldron of Blood

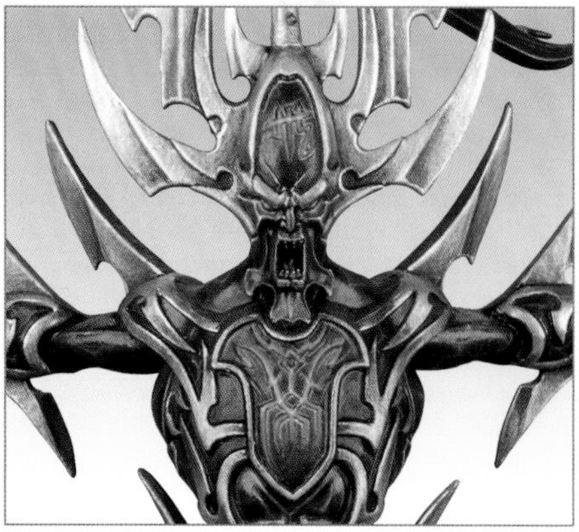

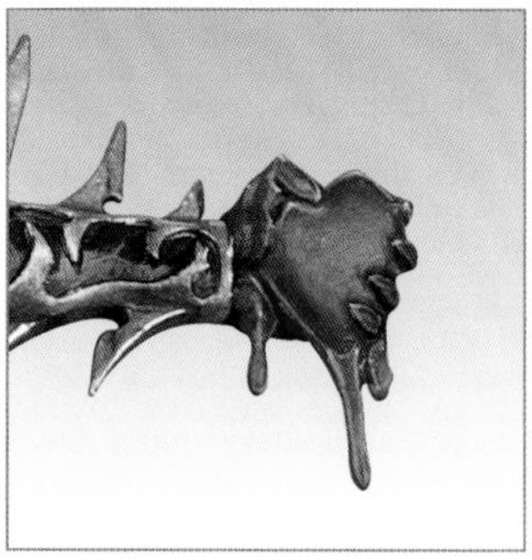

Khainite Shadowstalkers appear as if from nowhere to ambush and destroy a mob of rampaging Ironjawz.

Even as they charge at headlong pace, Doomfire Warlocks hurl bolts of foul sorcery at their foes.

Not even daemons are immune to the agonising aura that emanates from a Bloodwrack Shrine.

Shryke

Khinerai Heartrender

There are few warriors who have mastered the art of hit-and-run warfare more completely than the Khinerai, who take cruel delight in swooping down to hack and slice at their prey before retreating into the sky.

Khinerai Lifetaker *Harridynn* *Khinerai Lifetaker*

Shroud Queen Darkflame Warlock Shroudblade Darkflame Warlock

Khainite Shadowstalkers

Hag

Witch Aelves

Witch Aelf Standard Bearer

Hagg Nar
Hag

Kraith
Sister of Slaughter

Khailebron
Witch Aelf

Draichi Ganeth
Witch Aelf

Khelt Nar
Witch Aelf

There are no foes that the Daughters of Khaine fear, not even the living mountains of flesh known as Sons of Behemat – the bigger the sacrifice, the more blood for their ever-demanding god.

FURY OF HAGG NAR

Having ascended to godhood in a storm of blood and sacrifice, the goddess Morathi finds herself flushed with destructive power. Now, when her Daughters of Khaine march to war, they know that they do so alongside their deity made flesh – this only makes them more terrible opponents to face in battle.

You should feel free to collect your Daughters of Khaine army in any way that you wish. If you feel drawn to a massed horde of dagger-wielding Witch Aelves, that is just as viable an option as an elite force of cold-hearted Melusai or a swift-moving combination of Khinerai and Doomfire Warlocks. The army shown below is just one example of a coherent, themed army intended to inspire your own collection.

We have chosen to assemble a great war coven from Hagg Nar, the first and foremost temple of Khaine. And who better to lead such a force than the newly risen goddess Morathi? We are taking advantage of the rules presented within this battletome to field both Morathi-Khaine and the fearsome Shadow Queen at once. The split aspects of Morathi provide an incredibly potent combination of sorcery and raw, physical might. Morathi-Khaine is a peerless sorceress, wielding the magic of Ulgu with devastating effect and inspiring her flock to gruesome acts of violence. The Shadow Queen, by contrast, is an entity of sheer destruction that can carve her way through multiple enemy units. The Iron Heart of Khaine ensures both will survive the early battle rounds intact – to the horror of their foes.

The core of our army consists of Sisters of Slaughter and Witch Aelves, both deadly close-combat experts who boast a potent offence, only bolstered by the presence of a Hag Queen – a High Priestess of Khaine who leads her flock in bloody battle rites. Further bolstering the centre of the battle line, as well as providing its own offensive punch, is a Cauldron of Blood. This rolling war

12

10

2

1

6

8

shrine offers magical enhancements to nearby warriors, while the Slaughter Queen atop it deals out death with her razor-sharp blades.

Our elite troops come in the form of one unit of Blood Sisters and another of Blood Stalkers. The former are fearsome melee experts, capable of hewing their way through most targets put in front of them. The latter provide us with invaluable ranged firepower, peppering our foes with lethal arrows. This Scáthborn contingent is led by a Melusai Ironscale, a potent champion capable of shrugging off enemy magic.

This is a deadly core for any army, but to improve our ability to manoeuvre about the battlefield and seize important objectives, we need some swift, fast-attack units.

Fortunately, the Daughters of Khaine have several excellent options here. A unit of Doomfire Warlocks acts as light cavalry, able to cross the battlefield quickly and respond to any emerging threats. They also pack a reasonable punch with their sorcerous bolt attacks.

Even more deadly are the Khinerai Lifetakers, flying warriors who can dart in and out of battle with impressive effect. Their equally dangerous counterparts, the Khinerai Heartrenders, are equipped with javelins that they hurl with pinpoint force.

With a terrifying capacity for dealing out damage and impressive manoeuvrability, our army will surely earn many bloody victories in the name of Khaine!

1. Morathi-Khaine
2. The Shadow Queen
3. Hag Queen
4. Slaughter Queen on Cauldron of Blood
5. Melusai Ironscale
6. Sisters of Slaughter
7. Witch Aelves
8. Blood Sisters
9. Blood Stalkers
10. Doomfire Warlocks
11. Khinerai Lifetakers
12. Khinerai Heartrenders

'Hear me, my sisters, and I will tell you the one truth that matters: power. We have all felt the taint of what happens to those who are defeated, and it must never happen again. Rise, my Scáthborn, for you are my will...'

\- Morathi addressing her Melusai

PAINTING YOUR DAUGHTERS OF KHAINE

A Daughters of Khaine army presents many opportunities to experiment with different skin tones, hair colours, textures and special effects. What follows here is a brief but straightforward guide, including key painting techniques and stage-by-stage walkthroughs to help you paint your war coven.

One of the most enjoyable aspects of the Games Workshop hobby is taking paint and brush and bringing your collection of Citadel Miniatures to life. Even a single model looks fantastic when carefully painted and based. However, nothing beats gathering your miniatures together into a fully painted tabletop army upon the field of battle and seeing the impressive spectacle they present.

Painting your Citadel Miniatures is as much a personalised experience as collecting and gaming. Within the pages of this battletome and beyond, you will see many colour schemes that, should you choose to, you can copy in order to have your Daughters of Khaine hail from a specific temple. On the other hand, perhaps you would prefer to use your own palette and paint your models in colours that appeal to you.

Some painters enjoy lavishing hours of attention upon every model, bringing them up to the most spectacular individual standard they can manage. Others prefer to paint their models in batches, aiming to turn out entire regiments ready for battle whose coherent colour scheme and massed numbers make them look fantastic upon the tabletop. As with all aspects of this hobby, there's really no right or wrong way to do things so long as you're happy with the end result.

So embrace your creativity, get some paint on your brush and enjoy creating your own bloodthirsty war coven of Khainites!

WARHAMMER TV

Warhammer TV's painting tutorials have insights for everyone as they show you how to paint Citadel Miniatures from start to finish. The guides are available for free on games-workshop.com and can also be watched via the Warhammer TV YouTube channel. Why not take a moment to check them out?

MORATHI'S SKIN

1

Basecoat the skin with Rakarth Flesh.

2

Apply a shade of Reikland Fleshshade.

3

Layer the skin with Rakarth Flesh, making sure to avoid the recesses.

4

Carefully highlight with Pallid Wych Flesh.

5

Apply a shade of Carroburg Crimson to the lips. Paint the eyes with Rhinox Hide then White Scar, avoiding the recesses. Paint the pupils with Abaddon Black.

Gold: Basecoat with Balthasar Gold and shade with Reikland Fleshshade. Apply a layer of Gehenna's Gold followed by a layer of Liberator Gold. Finish with a sharp highlight of Stormhost Silver.

Black Hair: Basecoat with Abaddon Black. Apply progressively thinner highlights of Eshin Grey, Dawnstone and Administratum Grey.

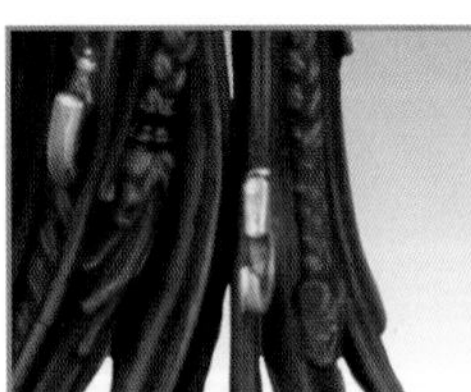

Snake Braids: Basecoat with Incubi Darkness, layer with Kabalite Green and highlight with Sybarite Green.

MORATHI'S ROBES

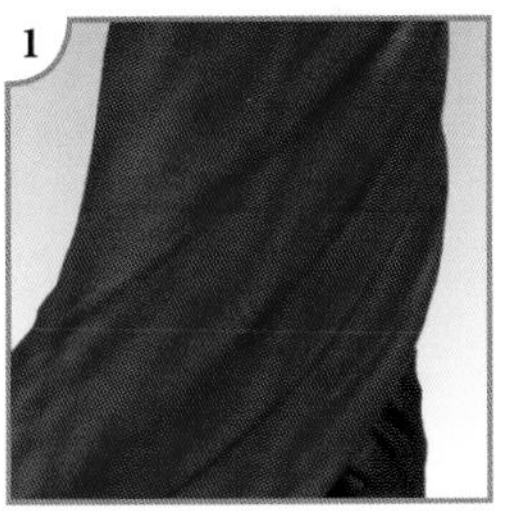

Apply a basecoat of Khorne Red.

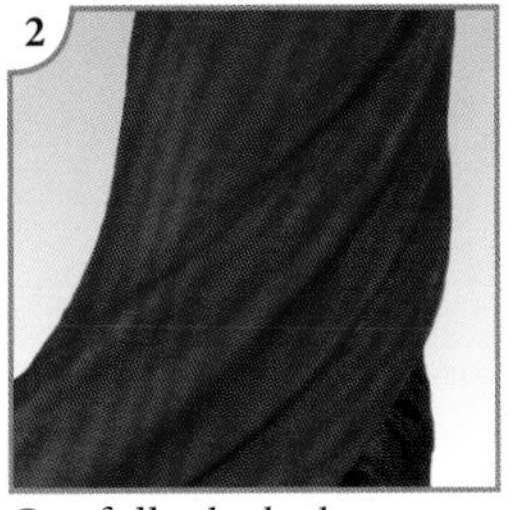

Carefully shade the recesses of the cloth with Nuln Oil.

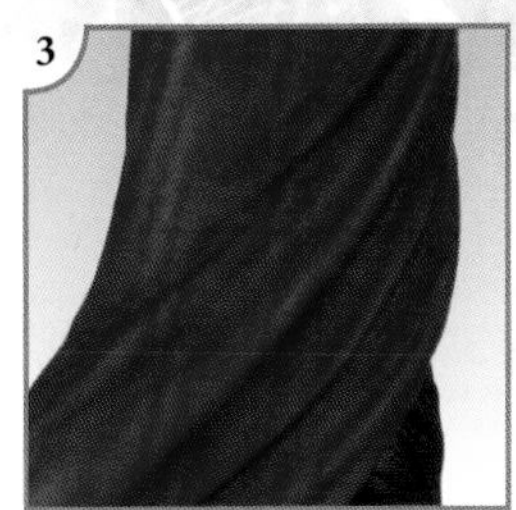

Apply a chunky highlight of Wazdakka Red to the edges of the folds.

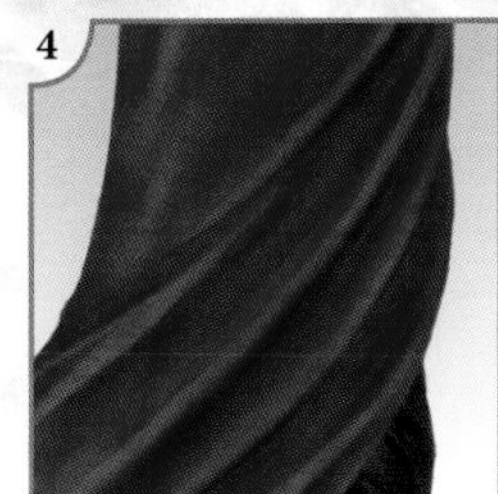

Apply a fine highlight of Tuskgor Fur.

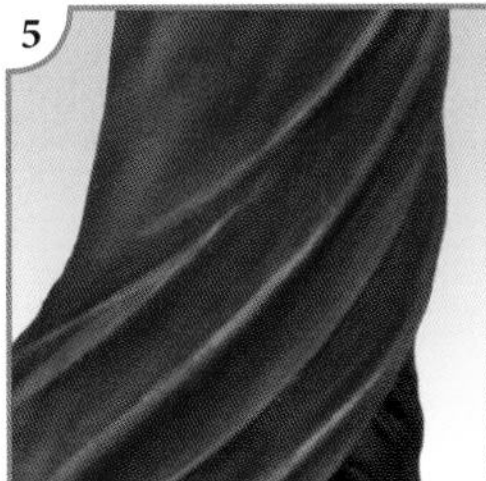

Finish with an even thinner highlight of Cadian Fleshtone.

Bright Red: Basecoat with Mephiston Red, add Nuln Oil to recesses, layer with Evil Sunz Scarlet, Fire Dragon Bright highlights.

Blood: Basecoat with Mephiston Red and then apply Blood For The Blood God.

TOP TIP:

It's good practice to give your painted miniatures a coat of Munitorum Varnish spray (following the instructions on the can) or Stormshield.

This will add an extra level of protection against the inevitable wear and tear of battle!

DRAICHI GANETH

Cloth: Basecoat with Mephiston Red, shade with Agrax Earthshade, then highlight with Evil Sunz Scarlet and Fire Dragon Bright.

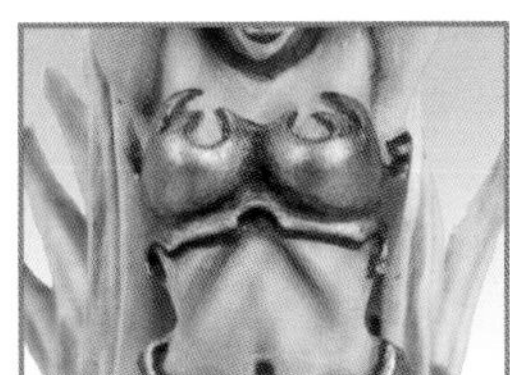
Armour: Basecoat with Ironbreaker, shade with Nuln Oil and highlight with Runefang Steel.

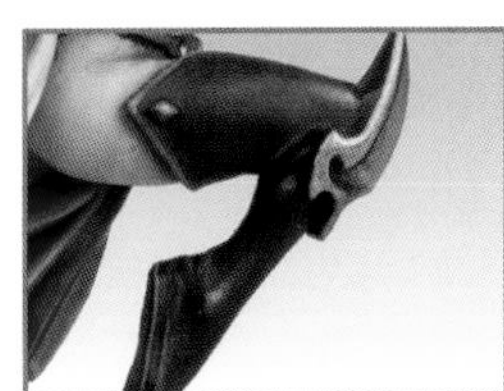
Black Leather: Basecoat with Abaddon Black, then highlight with Eshin Grey and Dawnstone.

Sisters of Slaughter Leather: Basecoat with Abaddon Black, then add Stegadon Scale Green and Sotek Green highlights.

Pink Hair: Basecoat with Corax White, apply a 1:1 mix of Druchii Violet and Lahmian Medium, then highlight with White Scar.

Green Hair: Basecoat with Corax White, shade the recesses with thinned Baharroth Blue and highlight with White Scar.

Melusai Bow: Basecoat with Abaddon Black, then highlight with Incubi Darkness and Sotek Green.

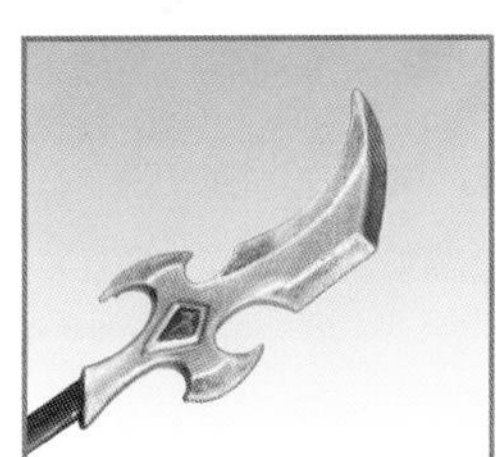
Glaive: Basecoat with Ironbreaker, shade with Coelia Greenshade and highlight with Stormhost Silver.

CONTRAST SKIN TONE

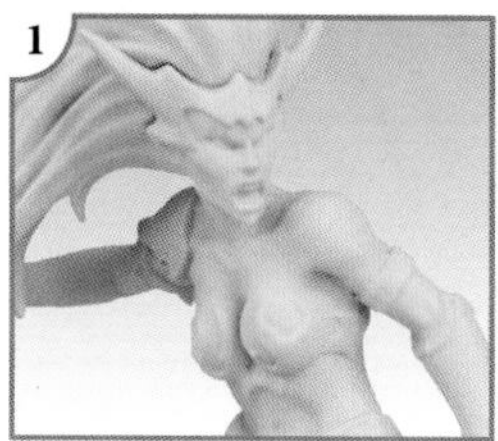

Undercoat the model with Wraithbone spray.

Apply a 1:1 mix of Guilliman Flesh and Contrast Medium.

Apply a layer of Wraithbone.

Finally, highlight with Pallid Wych Flesh.

DARK SKIN TONE

Apply a basecoat of Catachan Fleshtone.

Apply a layer of Bloodreaver Flesh, avoiding the recesses.

Apply a chunky highlight of Knight-Questor Flesh.

Finally, apply a fine highlight of Cadian Fleshtone.

FLUSHED SKIN TONE

Undercoat the model with Wraithbone spray.

Use a 1:4 mix of Carroburg Crimson and Lahmian Medium to shade the entire area.

Apply a layer of Pallid Wych Flesh, avoiding the recesses.

Add a highlight of White Scar.

ZAINTHAR KAI

Gold: Basecoat with Retributor Armour, shade with Reikland Fleshshade and highlight with Stormhost Silver. Carefully shade the recesses with Druchii Violet.

Cloth: Basecoat with Abaddon Black, then add a layer of Naggaroth Night, avoiding the recesses. Carefully highlight with Xereus Purple and Kakophoni Purple.

Hair: Basecoat with Abaddon Black, then add a layer of Barak-Nar Burgundy, avoiding the recesses. Highlight with Screamer Pink and Pink Horror.

Glaive: Basecoat with Ironbreaker and shade with Druchii Violet. Apply a fine highlight of Stormhost Silver.

KHAILEBRON

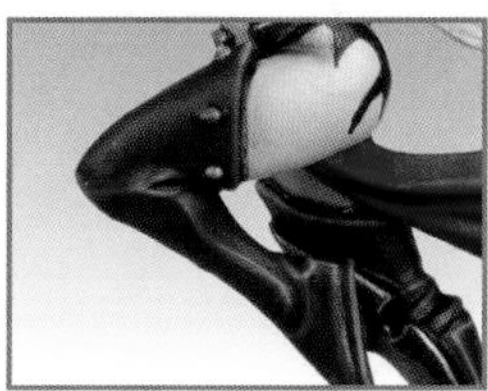
Leather: Kantor Blue (basecoat), Nuln Oil (shade), Temple Guard Blue and Fenrisian Grey (highlights)

Armour: Warplock Bronze (basecoat), Agrax Earthshade Gloss (shade), Ironbreaker (highlight)

Use Abaddon Black to carefully add tattoos and battle markings.

Glaive: Warplock Bronze (basecoat), Agrax Earthshade Gloss (shade), Ironbreaker (highlight)

HAGG NAR

Cloth: Khorne Red (basecoat), Nuln Oil (shade), Wazdakka Red and Wild Rider Red (highlights)

Hair: Corax White (basecoat), 1:1 Emperor's Children/Lahmian Medium (shade), 1:1 Wazdakka Red/Lahmian Medium (towards head)

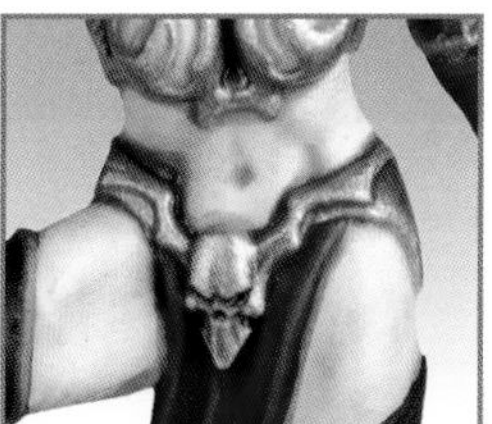
Gold: Retributor Gold (basecoat), Agrax Earthshade Gloss (shade), Runefang Steel (highlight)

Glaive: Ironbreaker (basecoat), Drakenhof Nightshade (shade), Stormhost Silver (highlight)

THE KRAITH

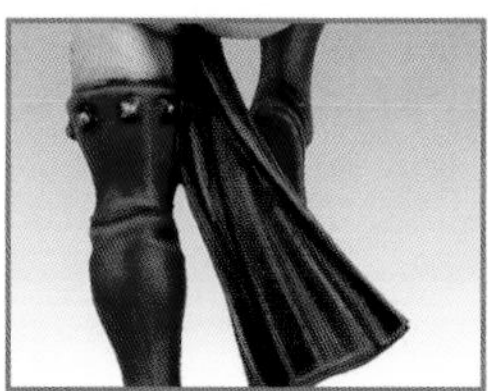
Cloth: Abaddon Black (basecoat), Mechanicus Standard Grey and Administratum Grey (highlights)

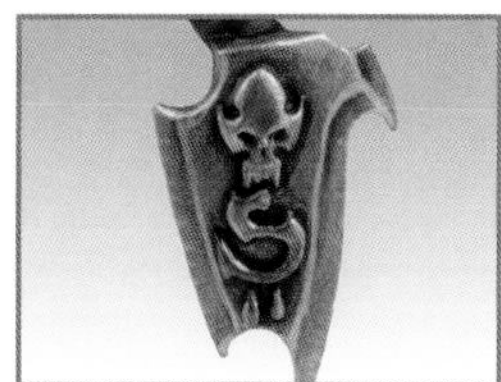
Armour: Leadbelcher (basecoat), Coelia Greenshade (shade), Runefang Steel (highlight)

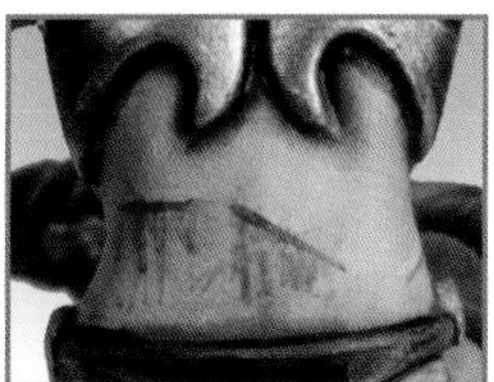
Wounds: Paint the cuts with Pink Horror and apply Blood For The Blood God.

Leather: Screamer Pink (basecoat), Nuln Oil (shade), Pink Horror and Emperor's Children (highlights)

KHELT NAR

Cloth: Abaddon Black (basecoat), Mechanicus Standard Grey and Administratum Grey (highlights)

Leather: Mephiston Red (basecoat), Agrax Earthshade (shade), Fire Dragon Bright (highlight)

Armour: Abaddon Black (basecoat), Retributor Gold around the edges and Runefang Steel (highlight)

Hair: Paint the same way as the cloth. Streak with Khorne Red, Wazdakka Red and Wild Rider Red.

MELUSAI SCALES

Crimson Scales: Basecoat with Mephiston Red, shade with Agrax Earthshade, then lightly drybrush with Kindleflame.
Black Scales: Simply basecoat with Abaddon Black and carefully edge highlight with The Fang.
Orange Scales: Basecoat with Jokaero Orange, shade with Reikland Fleshshade, then edge highlight with Bestigor Flesh.

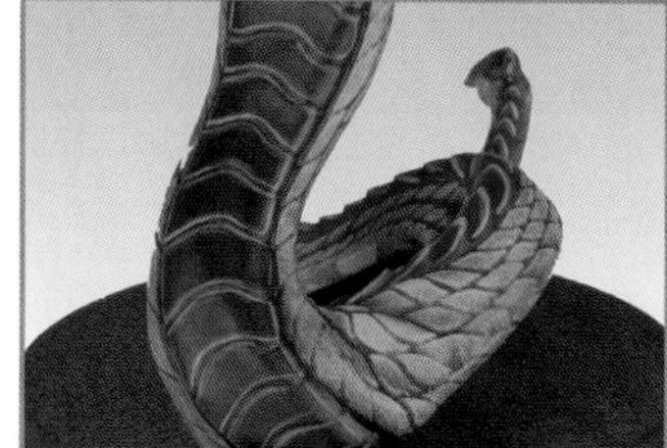

Turquoise Scales: Undercoat with Corax White spray, shade with Coelia Greenshade and drybrush with Skink Blue.
Purple Scales: Basecoat with Abaddon Black and highlight with Xereus Purple then Warpfiend Grey.
Fiery Red Scales: Basecoat with Khorne Red, shade with Nuln Oil and highlight with Evil Sunz Scarlet then Fire Dragon Bright.

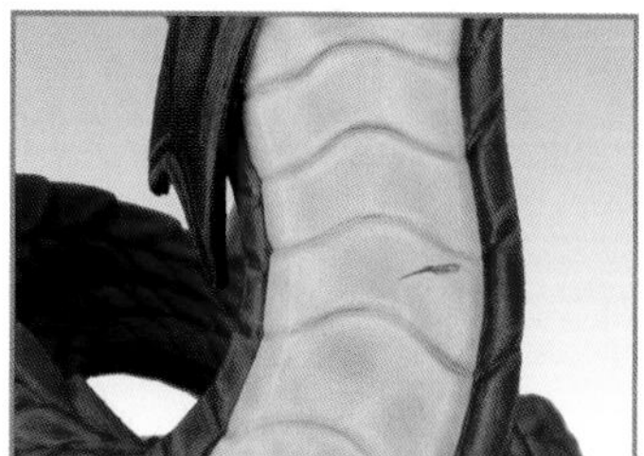

Pink Scales: Paint these using the same method as for Flushed Skin Tone.
Red Scales: Basecoat with Khorne Red, shade with Druchii Violet and highlight with Wazdakka Red and Wild Rider Red.

KHINERAI WINGS

Membrane: Basecoat with Khorne Red and apply a recess shade of Nuln Oil. Highlight with Wazdakka Red, then apply a final highlight of Wild Rider Red.
Claws: Basecoat with Ushabti Bone, shade with Seraphim Sepia, and then highlight with Screaming Skull. Apply a final highlight of Pallid Wych Flesh.

Membrane: Basecoat with Abaddon Black. Next, apply a highlight of Xereus Purple, then Warpfiend Grey, and then a fine highlight of Emperor's Children on the extremities.
Claws: Basecoat with Abaddon Black. Highlight with Kabalite Green and then apply a second highlight of Administratum Grey.

THE SHADOW QUEEN'S WINGS

Basecoat with Grey Seer and shade with Carroburg Crimson. Apply a couple of coats of Volupus Pink towards the fingers to create a darker blend. Drybrush the membrane with Grey Seer and very lightly with White Scar.

BANNER DESIGN

Carefully sketch out a diamond shape with Celestra Grey

Next, add a vertical line down the centre of the diamond.

Add two diagonal lines at the base of the diamond, forming a cross.

Add two more vertical lines, slightly curved, to finish the design.

BLOODY BLADES

To add smears of gore to weapons and armour, gently flick the surface with Rhinox Hide before liberally applying Blood For The Blood God.

CAULDRON OF BLOOD

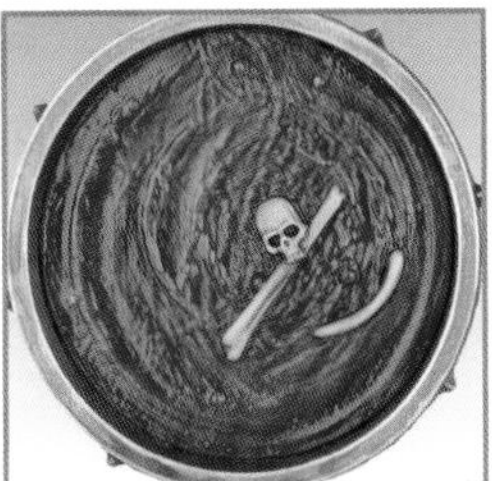

Basecoat with Mephiston Red, then apply an all-over shade of Agrax Earthshade. Drybrush with Evil Sunz Scarlet to pick out the texture before adding a highlight of Fire Dragon Bright. To finish, apply 'Ardcoat for a glossy sheen.

BLOODSHARDS AND HEARTS

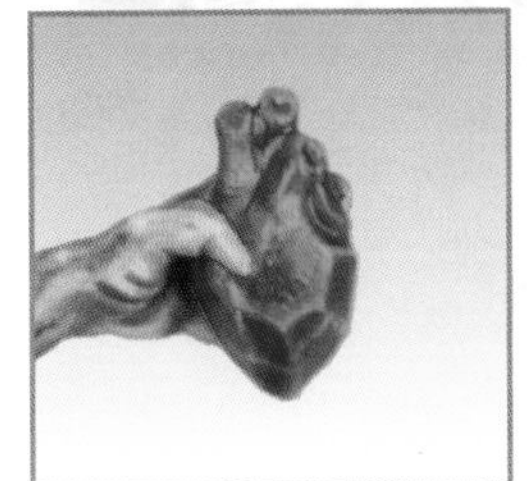

Begin with a basecoat of Khorne Red. Edge highlight with Evil Sunz Scarlet, then further bring out the details with Fire Dragon Bright. To finish, apply an all-over coat of 'Ardcoat.

AVATAR OF KHAINE

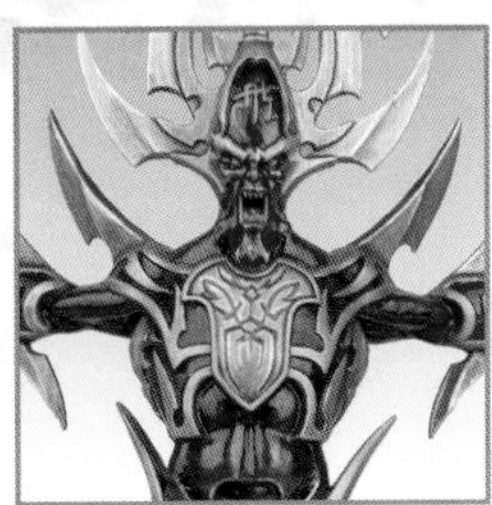

Paint the gold areas using one of the methods for Gold detailed previously in this guide. Then, add a liberal coat of Blood For The Blood God to the areas you wish to be red.

SISTERS OF SLAUGHTER MASKS

Basecoat with Retributor Armour. Apply a thinned shade of Blood For The Blood God to the recesses, and tidy up the flat areas with more Retributor Armour. Finally, highlight with Stormhost Silver.

Basecoat with Ironbreaker, then shade the recesses with Drakenhof Nightshade. Next, shade with Soulstone Blue thinned with Lahmian Medium. To finish, edge highlight with Stormhost Silver.

Basecoat with Khorne Red, then apply an all-over shade of Nuln Oil. Layer with Evil Sunz Scarlet, avoiding the shaded areas, and finish off with a highlight of Fire Dragon Bright.

Basecoat with Abaddon Black, then layer with Naggaroth Night, avoiding the recesses. Highlight with Xereus Purple and Kakophoni Purple.

BLOODWRACK SHRINE MIRROR GLASS

To begin, basecoat the mirror with Celestra Grey.

Apply a 1:1 mix of Coelia Greenshade and Lahmian Medium around the edge of the mirror, then lightly dapple this mix onto its surface, building up the colour on one side so that you get a smooth transition from light to dark.

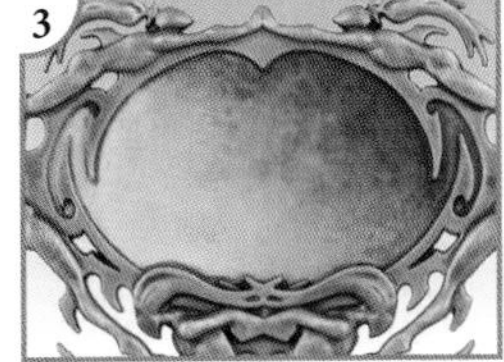

Next, thin down some Ulthuan Grey with Lahmian Medium and carefully apply a few thin coats to the lighter side of the mirror.

Finally, apply 'Ardcoat across the entire area for a shiny finish.

FORCES OF KHAINE

This battletome contains all of the rules you need to field your Daughters of Khaine miniatures on the battlefields of the Mortal Realms, from a host of exciting allegiance abilities to a range of warscrolls and warscroll battalions. The rules are split into the following sections:

ALLEGIANCE ABILITIES
This section describes the allegiance abilities available to a Daughters of Khaine army. The rules for using allegiance abilities can be found in the *Warhammer Age of Sigmar Core Book*.

BATTLE TRAITS
Abilities available to every unit in a Daughters of Khaine army (pg 61).

COMMAND TRAITS
Abilities available to the general of a Daughters of Khaine army if it is a **HERO** (pg 62-63).

ARTEFACTS OF POWER
Artefacts available to **HEROES** in a Daughters of Khaine army (pg 64-65).

SPELL LORES
Spells available to **WIZARD HEROES** in a Daughters of Khaine army (pg 66).

PRAYERS
Prayers available to **PRIESTS** in a Daughters of Khaine army (pg 67).

TEMPLES OF KHAINE
Abilities for the six most feared Khainite sects (pg 68-73). These rules can be used by units in a Daughters of Khaine army that have been given the appropriate keyword (see the Temples of Khaine battle trait).

BATTLEPLANS
This section includes a new narrative battleplan that can be played with a Daughters of Khaine army (pg 74-75).

PATH TO GLORY
This section contains rules for using your Daughters of Khaine collection in Path to Glory campaigns (pg 76-79).

WARSCROLLS
This section includes all of the warscrolls you will need to play games of Warhammer Age of Sigmar with your Daughters of Khaine miniatures. The following types of warscroll are included in this section:

WARSCROLL BATTALIONS
These are formations made up of several Daughters of Khaine units that combine their strengths to gain powerful new abilities (pg 80-83).

WARSCROLLS
A warscroll for each unit is included here. The rules for using a Daughters of Khaine unit, along with its characteristics and abilities, are detailed on its warscroll (pg 84-101).

ENDLESS SPELL WARSCROLLS
These warscrolls detail the rules for two unique and powerful endless spells that can be summoned by **WIZARDS** in a Daughters of Khaine army (pg 102). The rules for playing games with endless spells can be found in the *Warhammer Age of Sigmar Core Book* and in *Malign Sorcery*.

INVOCATION OF KHAINE WARSCROLL
This warscroll details the rules for a powerful invocation that can be used by **PRIESTS** in a Daughters of Khaine army (pg 103).

PITCHED BATTLE PROFILES
This section contains Pitched Battle profiles for the units, warscroll battalions, endless spells and invocations in this book (pg 104).

ALLIES
This section lists the allies a Daughters of Khaine army can include (pg 104).

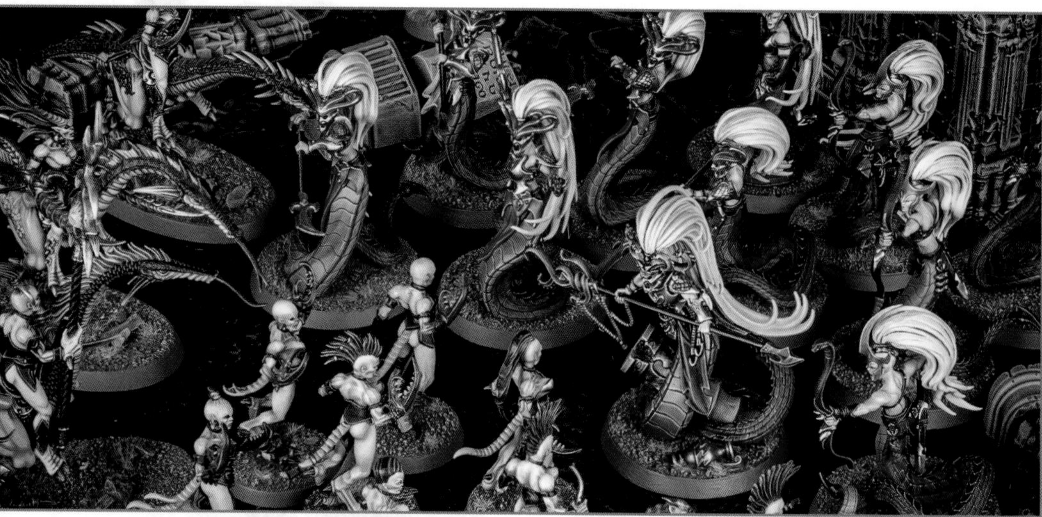

ALLEGIANCE ABILITIES

BATTLE TRAITS

APOSTLES OF THE MURDER GOD

BLOOD RITES

Before battle, the Daughters of Khaine are led by their priestesses in holy rites of bloodletting. With each gory sacrifice, the faithful are imbued with a fraction of their god's furious power.

Friendly **DAUGHTERS OF KHAINE** units gain an ability each battle round, as shown below. Note that the abilities are cumulative: units have the abilities of the current battle round and each previous battle round.

Battle Round	Ability
1	**Quickening Bloodlust:** *As battlelines are drawn, the hearts of Khaine's followers thump harder and their strides grow longer as they anticipate the battle to come.* You can re-roll run rolls of 1 for this unit.
2	**Headlong Fury:** *Reciting the catechism of Crimson Hate, the Khainites rush forwards in their eagerness to begin the slaughter.* You can re-roll rolls of 1 when making charge rolls for this unit.
3	**Zealot's Rage:** *The faithful chant the seventeen secret names of Khaine as they vent their rage, drawing the spirit of their murderous god to the battlefield.* You can re-roll hit rolls of 1 for attacks made with melee weapons by this unit. In addition, friendly **AVATARS OF KHAINE** are automatically animated (see the model's warscroll).
4	**Slaughterer's Strength:** *Having anointed their blades with the foe's blood, Khaine's flock are imbued with shocking strength.* You can re-roll wound rolls of 1 for attacks made with melee weapons by this unit.
5	**Unquenchable Fervour:** *With due sacrifice offered, the faithful are gripped by a vision that banishes mortal fears and pain instantly.* You can re-roll save rolls of 1 for attacks that target this unit. In addition, do not take battleshock tests for this unit.

FANATICAL FAITH

Their belief that their god will protect them is so powerful that the Daughters of Khaine can seemingly ignore mortal injuries.

Roll a dice each time a wound or mortal wound is allocated to a friendly **DAUGHTERS OF KHAINE** model. On a 6, that wound or mortal wound is negated.

TEMPLES OF KHAINE

There are a number of different sects dedicated to Khaine, each fixated on a different aspect of their patron and each maintaining its own great temple. All bow before Morathi, but as each sect strives to hold the greater part of their god's favour, rivalries are inevitable.

When you choose a Daughters of Khaine army, you can give it a Temple of Khaine keyword from the list below. All **DAUGHTERS OF KHAINE** units in your army gain that keyword, and you can use the allegiance abilities listed for that Temple of Khaine on the page indicated.

- **HAGG NAR** (pg 68)
- **DRAICHI GANETH** (pg 69)
- **KRAITH** (pg 70)
- **KHAILEBRON** (pg 71)
- **KHELT NAR** (pg 72)
- **ZAINTHAR KAI** (pg 73)

If a unit already has a Temple of Khaine keyword on its warscroll, it cannot gain another one. This does not preclude you from including the unit in your army, but you cannot use the allegiance abilities for its Temple of Khaine.

COMMAND TRAITS

PARAGONS OF MURDER

DAUGHTERS OF KHAINE AELF general only.

D6	Command Trait
1	**Bathed in Blood:** *This general bathes in sacrificial blood before battle, rejuvenating her and granting her healing powers.* Add 1 to this general's Wounds characteristic. In addition, at the start of your hero phase, you can heal 1 wound allocated to this general.
2	**Zealous Orator:** *This general is a skilled demagogue whose fiery oratory and utter disdain for weakness inspires her followers to fight on in the face of impossible odds.* Add 2 to the Bravery characteristic of friendly DAUGHTERS OF KHAINE units while they are wholly within 12" of this general.
3	**Sacrificial Overseer:** *This general has sacrificed countless victims upon the altars of her temple, and she is just as adept at offering lives to Khaine on the battlefield.* Add 1 to hit rolls for attacks made with melee weapons by this general.
4	**Terrifying Beauty:** *This general is possessed of a supernatural beauty that both enchants and terrifies her foes.* Subtract 1 from hit rolls for attacks that target this general.
5	**Master of Poisons:** *This general has intimate knowledge of all poisons and coats her blades in an elixir that can kill a warrior with the merest scratch.* Add 1 to the damage inflicted by each successful attack made by this general.
6	**True Believer:** *This general truly believes that she has been chosen for greatness, a conceit from which she draws great strength.* Add 1 to the number of the current battle round when determining the abilities gained by this general from the Blood Rites battle trait (pg 61). This ability and other similar abilities are cumulative.

MASTERS OF BLOOD MAGIC

Bloodwrack Medusa general only.

D3	Command Trait
1	**Arcane Mastery:** *This sorceress weaves strands of arcane energy into perfectly formed spells.* In your hero phase, you can re-roll 1 casting, dispelling or unbinding roll for this general.
2	**Writhing Coils:** *This Medusa uses slithering movements to confuse and trap her prey.* Subtract 1 from hit rolls for attacks that target this general.
3	**Fearsome Presence:** *This general radiates an aura of ruthless capability.* You can re-roll failed battleshock tests for friendly **Daughters of Khaine** units while they are wholly within 12" of this general.

MORATHI'S RIGHT HAND

Melusai Ironscale general only.

D3	Command Trait
1	**Veteran of the Cathtrar Dhule:** *This Ironscale has commanded her forces in the fiercest of battles.* If this general is part of your army and on the battlefield at the start of your hero phase, roll a dice. On a 4+, you receive 1 extra command point.
2	**Impenetrable Scales:** *Even honed blades find it all but impossible to penetrate this Melusai's form.* Add 1 to save rolls for attacks that target this general.
3	**Fuelled by Revenge:** *This general inspires a wrathful lust for vengeance in her warriors.* Once per battle, in your hero phase, you can use the Wrath of the Scáthborn command ability on this general's warscroll without spending any command points.

ARTEFACTS OF POWER

GIFTS OF MORATHI

Daughters of Khaine Hero only.

D6	Artefact of Power
1	**Crown of Woe:** *Forged from the cult of Khaine's first sacrificial altar, an aura of dread surrounds the wearer of this baleful crown.* Subtract 2 from the Bravery characteristic of enemy units while they are within 7" of the bearer. In addition, if any enemy models are slain by wounds inflicted by the bearer's attacks, increase the range of this ability to 14" for the remainder of the battle.
2	**Shadracar's Fang:** *Carved from a tooth of the legendary Umbral Dragon, this sword drains the colour and life from those it strikes, turning them into a formless shade.* Pick 1 of the bearer's melee weapons. Add 1 to hit rolls for attacks made with that weapon. In addition, if the unmodified hit roll for an attack made with that weapon is 6, the target suffers 1 mortal wound in addition to any normal damage.
3	**Amulet of Dark Fire:** *This amulet wreathes the wearer in flames that burn magic, granting powerful protection against spells.* Roll a dice each time you allocate a mortal wound to the bearer that was inflicted by a spell. On a 4+, that mortal wound is negated.
4	**Crone Blade:** *As a Crone Blade drinks deep of its victims' lifeblood, its wielder grows visibly younger before her enemies' very eyes, her vigour and murderlust restored.* Pick 1 of the bearer's melee weapons. At the end of the combat phase, if any enemy models were slain by wounds inflicted by attacks made with that weapon in that phase, you can heal up to D3 wounds allocated to the bearer.
5	**Thousand and One Dark Blessings:** *Upon this champion, Morathi herself has bestowed blessings of preservation woven from shadow.* Roll a dice each time you allocate a wound or mortal wound to the bearer. On a 5+, that wound or mortal wound is negated.
6	**Bloodbane Venom:** *One of the wielder's blades is coated with a deadly poison that causes even the tiniest wound to bleed openly and profusely, exsanguinating the victim in seconds.* Pick 1 of the bearer's melee weapons. At the end of the combat phase, if any wounds inflicted by attacks made with that weapon in that phase were allocated to an enemy model and not negated, and that enemy model has not been slain, roll a dice. If the roll is equal to or greater than that model's Wounds characteristic, that model is slain.

ARTEFACTS OF SHADOW

Bloodwrack Medusa only.

D6 Artefact of Power

1 **Shadow Stone:** *Crafted in another age from a piece of darkest realmstone, this unassuming item grants the bearer mastery of shadow magic.*

Add 1 to casting rolls for the bearer.

2 **Rune of Ulgu:** *This sorceress is marked with the ever-shifting rune of Ulgu, granting them innate knowledge of the shadow magic that saturates the realm.*

The bearer knows 1 extra spell from the Lore of Shadows (pg 66).

3 **The Mirror Glaive:** *The blade of this glaive is crafted from polished realmglass; in skilled hands, it can absorb and reflect the energy of enemy sorceries.*

Each time the bearer successfully unbinds a spell, they can immediately attempt to cast either the Arcane Bolt or Mystic Shield spell as if it were your hero phase. In addition, if the casting roll is successful, the spell cannot be unbound.

4 **Sevenfold Shadow:** *This wizard possesses a living shadow that can, at a command, envelop them and transport them across the shadow realm.*

Once per battle in your movement phase, instead of making a normal move with the bearer, you can remove the bearer from the battlefield and set them up again anywhere on the battlefield more than 9" from any enemy units.

5 **Crystal Heart:** *This mage's heart was turned to living crystal. Great magic resides within, but each time it is used, another crack appears...*

The bearer can attempt to cast 1 extra spell in your hero phase. If they do so, roll a dice before making the casting roll. On a 1, the bearer suffers D3 mortal wounds.

6 **Shade Claw:** *Dipped in the Stygian depths of a gloom lake, this claw slips in and out of reality, passing through armour as if it were nothing.*

The bearer's Whisperclaw has a Rend characteristic of -2.

RELICS OF KHAINE

Daughters of Khaine Priest only.

D6 Artefact of Power

1 **Blood Sigil:** *This token is inscribed with a mysterious sigil of power and entrusted to only the highest-ranking Khainites.*

The bearer knows 1 extra prayer from the Prayers of the Khainite Cult (pg 67).

2 **Iron Circlet:** *During its forging, this headband was quenched in the blood of a sacrificed Slaughter Queen so that her indomitable faith would forever bolster the wearer's.*

You can re-roll prayer rolls of 1 for the bearer.

3 **Rune of Khaine:** *Inscribed into the supplicant's forehead, it is said that Khaine's vengeance will find those who harm the bearer of this rune.*

The first time the bearer is slain by an attack, before removing them from the battlefield, roll a dice. On a 1, nothing happens. On a 2-5, the attacking unit suffers D3 mortal wounds. On a 6, the attacking unit suffers D6 mortal wounds.

4 **Crimson Shard:** *Rumoured to have been forged from a sliver of Khaine's own sword, this blade is amongst the cult's most holy artefacts.*

Pick 1 of the bearer's melee weapons. Add 2 to wound rolls for attacks made with that weapon by the bearer.

5 **Khainite Pendant:** *The wearer can call for Khaine's blessings as easily as drawing breath, but woe betide them if they are found unworthy.*

In your hero phase, the bearer can chant up to 3 prayers. If they do so, make a prayer roll for each by rolling a dice. However, on a 1, the bearer suffers D3 mortal wounds instead of 1 and the prayer is not answered.

6 **Hagbrew:** *Before battle, this priestess imbibes a draught of Hagbrew, entering a berserker trance.*

Add 1 to wound rolls for attacks made with melee weapons by the bearer.

SPELL LORES

You can choose or roll for 1 of the following spells for each **Wizard Hero** in a Daughters of Khaine army.

LORE OF SHADOWS

Daughters of Khaine Wizard Hero only.

D6	Spell
1	**Steed of Shadows:** *A coal-black creature with wings of night materialises from the darkness and swoops across the battlefield, carrying the caster swiftly above the fray.* Steed of Shadows has a casting value of 6. If successfully cast, until your next hero phase, the caster has a Move characteristic of 16" and can fly.
2	**Pit of Shades:** *The wizard opens a rift to the infamous Pit of Shades. Terrified warriors fall screaming through the portal, plummeting to a shadowy no-place filled with the incessant wailing of 'those who dwell beyond'.* Pit of Shades has a casting value of 7. If successfully cast, pick 1 enemy unit within 18" of the caster that is visible to them and roll 2D6. If the roll is higher than that unit's Move characteristic, that unit suffers a number of mortal wounds equal to the difference between its Move characteristic and the roll.
3	**Mirror Dance:** *The wizard casts a spell of shifting, revealing a shadowpath between two distant allies that allows them to move across the battlefield in a heartbeat.* Mirror Dance has a casting value of 6. If successfully cast, pick 2 friendly **Daughters of Khaine Heroes** wholly within 18" of the caster that are visible to them. Remove those **Heroes** from the battlefield and set them up again anywhere on the battlefield more than 9" from any enemy units. Those **Heroes** cannot move in the following movement phase.
4	**The Withering:** *The wizard plants overwhelmingly vivid images of frailty and doubt in their foes' minds.* The Withering has a casting value of 7. If successfully cast, pick 1 enemy unit within 18" of the caster that is visible to them. Add 1 to wound rolls for attacks that target that unit until your next hero phase.
5	**Mindrazor:** *The wizard summons spectral blades into their allies' hands, weapons whose edges are honed by the wielder's faith as much as the victim's fear.* Mindrazor has a casting value of 8. If successfully cast, pick 1 friendly **Daughters of Khaine** unit wholly within 18" of the caster. Improve the Rend characteristic of that unit's melee weapons by 1 until your next hero phase. In addition, until your next hero phase, add 1 to the Damage characteristic of that unit's melee weapons if it made a charge move in the same turn.
6	**Shroud of Despair:** *Numbing darkness descends upon the battlefield, suppressing the foe's will to fight.* Shroud of Despair has a casting value of 4. If successfully cast, pick 1 enemy unit within 18" of the caster that is visible to them. Subtract 1 from that unit's Bravery characteristic until your next hero phase. If the casting roll was 8+, subtract D3 from that unit's Bravery characteristic instead of 1 until your next hero phase.

PRAYERS

In your hero phase, each friendly **Daughters of Khaine Priest** that knows any prayers can chant each prayer that they know. If they do so, make a prayer roll by rolling a dice. On a 1, that **Priest** suffers 1 mortal wound and the prayer is not answered. On a 2, the prayer is not answered. On a 3+, the prayer is answered.

In addition to any other prayers they know, each friendly **Priest** in a Daughters of Khaine army knows 1 prayer from the Prayers of the Khainite Cult. You can either choose or roll for the prayer each **Priest** knows. Each prayer from the Prayers of the Khainite Cult can only be chanted once per turn, regardless of how many **Priests** know that prayer.

PRAYERS OF THE KHAINITE CULT

Daughters of Khaine Priest only.

D6 Prayer

1 **Catechism of Murder:** *Khaine's followers enter a killing frenzy that knows no bounds, lashing out in a slicing storm of razored steel that sees the ground become slick with the enemy's lifeblood.*

If this prayer is answered, pick 1 friendly **Daughters of Khaine** unit wholly within 14" of this model. Until your next hero phase, if the unmodified hit roll for an attack made with a melee weapon by that unit is 6, that attack scores 2 hits on the target instead of 1. Make a wound and save roll for each hit.

2 **Blessing of Khaine:** *Screaming her sisters' devotion to the skies, the priestess channels their faith into a potent aura of protection that turns aside the enemy's blows at the last moment.*

If this prayer is answered, pick 1 friendly **Daughters of Khaine** unit wholly within 14" of this model. Until your next hero phase, you can re-roll Fanatical Faith rolls (pg 61) for that unit.

3 **Martyr's Sacrifice:** *The priestess shrieks an oath of vengeance and spite, beseeching Khaine to give those faithful who have been struck down the strength to deliver one final blow.*

If this prayer is answered, pick 1 friendly **Daughters of Khaine** unit wholly within 14" of this model. Until your next hero phase, each time a model from that unit is slain by an attack made with a melee weapon, before the slain model is removed from play, pick 1 enemy unit within 3" of the slain model and roll a dice. On a 5+, that unit suffers 1 mortal wound.

4 **Crimson Rejuvenation:** *A coppery tang fills the air as a bloody mist with restorative powers surrounds Khaine's chosen, sealing their wounds in moments.*

If this prayer is answered, pick 1 friendly **Daughters of Khaine** unit wholly within 14" of this model. Heal up to D3 wounds allocated to that unit.

5 **Covenant of the Iron Heart:** *The hearts of the Murder God's followers become as cold and hard as iron, crushing their fears and doubts and replacing them with a chilling contempt for weakness.*

If this prayer is answered, pick 1 friendly **Daughters of Khaine** unit wholly within 14" of this model. Until your next hero phase, do not take battleshock tests for that unit.

6 **Sacrament of Blood:** *The dreaded rune of Khaine spontaneously manifests on the brows of the faithful as if carved there by some ghostly knife. Rivulets of blood run down their enraptured faces as they are saturated with the power of their deity.*

If this prayer is answered, pick 1 friendly **Daughters of Khaine** unit wholly within 14" of this model. Until your next hero phase, add 1 to the number of the current battle round when determining the abilities gained by that unit from the Blood Rites battle trait (pg 61). This ability and other similar abilities are cumulative.

HAGG NAR

None of the great sects of the Khainite cult can hope to rival mighty Hagg Nar in splendour or divine favour. Morathi's stronghold boasts the largest armies, the deadliest war engines and the most fervent warriors, each of whom longs for the opportunity to spill blood in the name of the ascended goddess.

In the aftermath of Morathi's rise to godhood, the power of Hagg Nar – already formidable – has only reached greater heights. Almost every hour, new hosts can be sighted marching forth from the iron towers of the First Temple, dispatched across the vast expanse of the Mortal Realms on missions of slaughter and sacrifice. Pride has never been lacking amongst those who hail from the Khainite capital, and – with some justification – they believe themselves to be blessed above all by their goddess Morathi. This surety makes them fight all the more ferociously, for the thought that they might be defeated cannot be countenanced.

Of all the sects, it is unquestionably Hagg Nar that fields the most holy relics – particularly Cauldrons of Blood, of which Morathi keeps many close at hand. Manned by Hag Queens drunk on the intoxicating power of Morathi-Khaine, these war-shrines form nexuses of faith for a Hagg Nar coven, around which flocks of battle-crazed Witch Aelves and Sisters of Slaughter fight and slay. Moreover, many fearsome Avatars of Khaine stride alongside the Hagg Nar war covens, given motion and fury by Morathi-Khaine and her High Priestesses.

ABILITIES

Daughters of the First Temple: *The proud warriors of Hagg Nar see themselves as the true inheritors of Khaine's power, and they strive to prove their worth when set upon the enemy.*

Add 1 to the number of the current battle round when determining the abilities gained by friendly HAGG NAR units from the Blood Rites battle trait (pg 61). This ability and other similar abilities are cumulative.

COMMAND ABILITY

Send Forth the Cauldrons: *The sacred cauldron shrines of Hagg Nar are driven forward with a murderous zeal by their honoured attendants.*

You can use this command ability at the start of your movement phase. If you do so, pick 1 friendly HAGG NAR CAULDRON OF BLOOD within 3" of any friendly HAGG NAR units that have 3 or more models and wholly within 12" of a friendly HAGG NAR HERO. Add 3" to the Move characteristic of that CAULDRON OF BLOOD until your next hero phase. The same unit cannot benefit from this command ability more than once per turn.

COMMAND TRAIT

A HAGG NAR general must have this command trait instead of one listed on pages 62-63.

Devoted Disciple: *The intensity and ferocity of faith displayed by the priestesses and sorcerers of Hagg Nar is daunting even to the sisters of other Khainite sects.*

The Fanatical Faith battle trait (pg 61) negates a wound allocated to a friendly HAGG NAR DAUGHTERS OF KHAINE model on a 5+ instead of a 6 while it is wholly within 12" of this general.

ARTEFACT OF POWER

The first HAGG NAR HERO to receive an artefact of power must be given the Ulfúri.

The Ulfúri: *The burning, crimson edge of this blade becomes ever more blazingly intense as it feeds upon the spilled gore of slain victims.*

Pick 1 of the bearer's melee weapons. Add 1 to the Damage characteristic of that weapon if the bearer made a charge move in the same turn.

DRAICHI GANETH

To all Daughters of Khaine, the act of dealing death is a form of worship, but none take part in ritualised slaughter with such artistic relish as those of Draichi Ganeth. Fearsome gladiators who seek to perfect their delivery of the killing blow, they take every opportunity to hone their skills on worthy foes.

Those of Draichi Ganeth seek victory not through cunning or manoeuvre but through perfectly honed combat skills. Before battle, they perform extravagant rites such as the Colmthart – the Dance of Scars – or the Thair'nik – the Crimson Mark. These rituals demonstrate the bladecraft of the she-aelves and foreshadow the manner in which they will defeat their foe. Once the enemy is vanquished in honourable combat, the Draichi Ganeth practise Krish'lar – the wearing of the foe's blood.

The first temple dedicated to the Draichi Ganeth can be found in the northern barrens of Fuarthorn in Ulgu, but this sect has spread further than any other. There are temples dedicated to this cult across each of the Mortal Realms, including a shrine in all of the major cities established during the Age of Sigmar.

Unsurprisingly, then, these Daughters of Khaine are the most commonly seen by the forces of Order. They revel in the attention brought by their ritual combat displays, yet such shows cannot match the exhilaration they feel when delivering the final blow to those who stand in their way.

ABILITIES

Bladed Killers: *Forged in the arena death-pits, those of Draichi Ganeth are among the most masterful warriors in the Mortal Realms.*

Improve the Rend characteristic of melee weapons used by friendly **DRAICHI GANETH WITCH AELVES** units and friendly **DRAICHI GANETH SISTERS OF SLAUGHTER** units by 1 if that unit made a charge move in the same turn.

COMMAND ABILITY

A Thousand Bladeforms: *So skilled are the warriors of Draichi Ganeth that they can alter their fighting style to overwhelm any foe.*

You can use this command ability in the combat phase. If you do so, pick 1 friendly **DRAICHI GANETH WITCH AELVES** unit or 1 friendly **DRAICHI GANETH SISTERS OF SLAUGHTER** unit wholly within 12" of a friendly **DRAICHI GANETH HERO**. Add 1 to hit rolls for attacks made with melee weapons by that unit until the end of that phase. The same unit cannot benefit from this command ability more than once per turn.

COMMAND TRAIT

A **DRAICHI GANETH** general must have this command trait instead of one listed on pages 62-63.

Victor of Yaith'ril: *This general has triumphed in the great blood-games contested between Draichi Ganeth and the hated Kraith, and she is held in the highest regard by her warriors.*

Add 1 to the Bravery characteristic of friendly **DRAICHI GANETH** units while they are wholly within 12" of this general.

ARTEFACT OF POWER

The first **DRAICHI GANETH HERO** to receive an artefact of power must be given Death's Kiss.

Death's Kiss: *Forged by the legendary swordsmith Taltresca, this blade's balance and cutting edge are both almost impossibly perfect.*

Pick 1 of the bearer's melee weapons. Add 2 to the Attacks characteristic of that weapon if the bearer made a charge move in the same turn.

THE KRAITH

The Kraith seek not only to defeat their foes but to bleed them to the last drop. For these crazed slaughterers, true worship of Khaine comes through the spilling of blood in truly gruesome quantities, and they employ their mastery of the lash and the blade in order to sate the Murder God's desire.

The warriors of the Kraith, also known as the Crimson Cult, are true disciples of slaughter, and they have earned a reputation as the least compromising of all the Daughters of Khaine. Their bloodthirsty post-battle rites have led to allies reneging on their compacts with the she-aelves out of sheer disgust and cause even the most stalwart Stormcast Eternals to shudder.

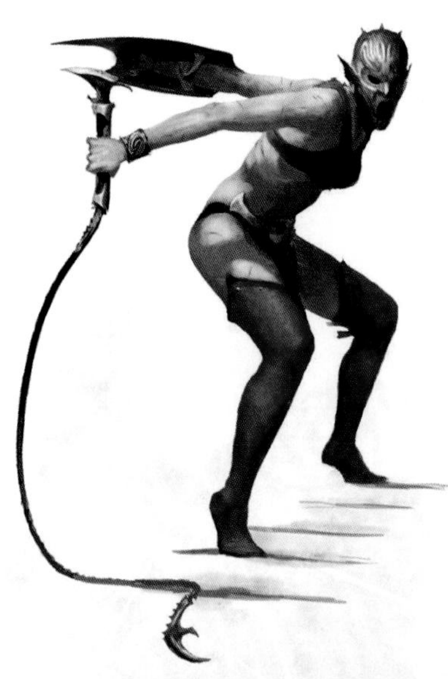

The Kraith do not maintain their own temples, for they believe the proper place to worship Khaine is the battlefield. Instead, they travel between the temples of other sects, hiring out their services clearing lands of monsters and fighting in gladiatorial arenas.

Those of the Kraith believe that all others are inferior, suited only to providing the blood in which they might bathe. They respond to insults or perceived slights with drawn blades, and their hot-tempered aggression has drawn censure from Hagg Nar more than once. Only their brutal effectiveness as unleashed killers has prevented Morathi from subjecting them to a more extreme punishment.

ABILITIES

Disciples of Slaughter: *The warriors of the Kraith refuse to cease their assault until every last drop of blood in the enemy's veins has been claimed.*

At the end of the combat phase, you can roll a dice for each friendly **KRAITH SISTERS OF SLAUGHTER** unit that fought once in that phase. On a 5+, that unit can fight for a second time.

COMMAND ABILITY

Inspired by Carnage: *The Kraith scorn subtlety in favour of the rush of slaughter, becoming increasingly frenzied with each eviscerated foe.*

You can use this command ability in the combat phase. If you do so, pick 1 friendly **KRAITH SISTERS OF SLAUGHTER** unit wholly within 12" of a friendly **KRAITH HERO**. Add 1 to wound rolls for attacks made by that unit in that phase. The same unit cannot benefit from this command ability more than once per phase.

COMMAND TRAIT

A **KRAITH** general must have this command trait instead of one listed on pages 62-63.

Bathe in Their Blood!: *Priestesses of the Kraith delight in goading their flock into an ever more terrible battle-frenzy, exulting in the ensuing displays of violence.*

At the end of the combat phase, if this general is on the battlefield and any enemy units were destroyed by attacks made by friendly **KRAITH** units in that phase, you receive 1 command point.

ARTEFACT OF POWER

The first **KRAITH HERO** to receive an artefact of power must be given the Venom of Nagendra.

Venom of Nagendra: *With a single drop of this potent venom, this Daughter causes her victims' blood to boil in their veins, killing them in an explosive instant.*

Pick 1 of the bearer's melee weapons. Once per battle, at the start of the combat phase, you can say that the bearer will anoint that weapon with the Venom of Nagendra. If you do so, pick 1 enemy unit within 1" of the bearer. That unit suffers D6 mortal wounds, but the bearer cannot fight with that melee weapon in that combat phase.

KHAILEBRON

Silent as shadows, as swift as death, the Khailebron stalk their prey. Warriors from this secretive sect strive to become pure manifestations of murder, eschewing grandiose displays and frontal assaults in favour of seeking out the enemy's weak points and thrusting a scianlar home with merciless precision.

The Khailebron have learnt well the arts of concealment, stealth and obfuscation. Those who worship at the shadow-shrouded temples of this sect revere the assassin and the unseen killer, and they strive to be masters of the ambush and the sudden strike. As a consequence, they are often tasked by Morathi to travel the realms on missions to deliver lethal messages on her behalf, both to enemies and to erstwhile allies. The Khailebron's war covens maintain a public facade as performing troupes of blade dancers and graceful pit fighters, but the sect's true rituals are kept well hidden from prying eyes.

The Khailebron arrive in battle shrouded by rolling banks of mist, and they revel in misdirection and illusion. Just when the enemy thinks they have seen the true threat, another attack strikes from an unexpected quarter to rip the heart out of their army. Although fairness and honour have never been pressing concerns amongst the Daughters of Khaine, the other sects – particularly Draichi Ganeth –are sometimes enraged by the Khailebron's underhanded tactics

ABILITIES

Concealment and Stealth: *Masked as they are by illusions and banks of shadow, the armies of the Khailebron are almost impossible to strike at range.*

Subtract 1 from hit rolls for attacks made with missile weapons that target friendly KHAILEBRON units.

COMMAND ABILITY

Masters of the Shadowpaths: *Few Khainites are as well versed in the secrets ways of the shadowpaths as those of the Khailebron, who can strike at their quarry where they least expect it.*

You can use this command ability at the end of your movement phase. If you do so, pick 1 friendly KHAILEBRON unit wholly within 12" of a friendly KHAILEBRON HERO that is a general. Remove that unit from the battlefield and set it up again anywhere on the battlefield more than 9" from any enemy units. That unit cannot move in the next movement phase.

COMMAND TRAIT

A KHAILEBRON general must have this command trait instead of one listed on pages 62-63.

Mistress of Illusion: *This general often toys with her prey, disappearing into the shadows only to re-emerge from an unseen vantage point.*

Subtract 1 from hit rolls for attacks made with melee weapons that target this general.

ARTEFACT OF POWER

The first KHAILEBRON HERO to receive an artefact of power must be given Whisperdeath.

Whisperdeath: *The blade of this weapon seems to be fashioned from a wisp of smoke, yet it can pierce almost any substance without resistance.*

Pick 1 of the bearer's melee weapons. If the unmodified hit roll for an attack made with that weapon is 6, that attack inflicts 1 mortal wound on the target in addition to any normal damage.

KHELT NAR

Bold and ambitious, the burgeoning sect of Khelt Nar has risen to dramatic prominence during the Age of Sigmar. Its master weaponsmiths possess the secrets of fashioning shadow-infused weapons, ornate blades and barbed whips that inflict a strange and debilitating curse in those they strike.

The foundations for Khelt Nar's growth were apparent from its very creation, for the Rothtor – the mountain atop which the sect's great temple of Ironshard was built – was itself a priceless deposit of shadow-infused metal. It was not long before Slaughter Queen artisans working under Morathi's guidance had perfected the art of turning this substance into deadly kuirath.

Khelt Nar armies make use of their most potent weapon by striking swiftly then fading back as the mind-scouring magic that permeates their weapons does its work. Enemies are soon left stumbling and reeling in a black cloud of confusion, barely able to raise their blades as the Khelt Nar warriors come rushing back in at them. Numerous Chaos hosts have met their bloody end through such tactics.

These hit-and-fade attacks are often led by swooping packs of Khinerai; the shrine of Ironshard is surrounded by dozens of brood-nest towers that encircle the mountainous stronghold like curling talons.

ABILITIES

Strike and Fade: *Warriors of Khelt Nar sink their cursed kuirath blades deep into the flesh of their foes, and when the enemy begins to reel in sickened confusion, the Khainites retreat and ready for a devastating follow-up charge.*

Friendly **KHELT NAR** units can retreat and still charge later in the same turn.

COMMAND ABILITY

Bleed the Mind: *Priestesses of Khelt Nar can empower the mind-fogging curse delivered by kuirath, rendering those afflicted so disoriented that they leave themselves open to a deadly riposte or even inflict deadly wounds upon themselves in their confusion.*

You can use this command ability at the start of the combat phase. If you do so, pick 1 friendly **KHELT NAR** unit wholly within 12" of a friendly **KHELT NAR HERO**. Until your next hero phase, if the unmodified hit roll for an attack made with a melee weapon that targets that **KHELT NAR** unit is 1, the attacking unit suffers 1 mortal wound after all of its attacks have been resolved.

COMMAND TRAIT

A **KHELT NAR** general must have this command trait instead of one listed on pages 62-63.

The Circling Flock: *The soaring flocks of Khinerai that follow the forces of Khelt Nar suddenly descend upon the battlefield from on high.*

Once per battle, at the end of your movement phase, you can say that this general will summon a flock of Khinerai to the battlefield. If you do so, you can add 1 **KHINERAI HARPIES** unit of 5 models to your army. Set up that unit anywhere on the battlefield more than 9" from any enemy units.

ARTEFACT OF POWER

The first **KHELT NAR HERO** to receive an artefact of power must be given Gáisa's Falx.

Gáisa's Falx: *This slightly hooked blade – the favoured weapon of a long-dead Hag Queen – can carve through metal and bone with ease, but its true power lies in the sinister, mind-shredding enchantments laid upon it.*

Pick 1 of the bearer's melee weapons. If the unmodified hit roll for an attack made with that weapon is 6, that attack scores 2 hits on the target instead of 1. Make a wound and save roll for each hit.

ZAINTHAR KAI

The Melusai shock troops of the Zainthar Kai are seen as nothing less than living saints by many Khainites, for each of these warriors carries in their veins no fewer than three drops of Khaine's holy blood – a cursed lineage that not only offers supernatural power but can also be turned into a potent weapon against the bearer's foes.

The origins of the Zainthar Kai hearken back to the days of the Cathtrar Dhule. Desperate for a winning weapon in the war against Chaos, Morathi created a new breed of Scáthborn, each of whom had at least three drops of Khaine's cursed blood in their veins. Most of these subjects died horribly, unable to bear such terrible potency. Those who survived learnt to wield the curse that coursed through their bodies as a weapon, calling upon its simmering power to strengthen their strikes and wrack their foes with unbearable agony. When lost in the throes of battle-frenzy, a Zainthar Kai broodcrone can even cause the lifeblood of nearby enemies to erupt from their eyes, nose and mouth in a boiling torrent.

For years, this highly isolationist and enigmatic sect has functioned as Morathi's secret weapon, destroying any foe that she wishes to be rid of. The sect is almost entirely composed of Scáthborn, though its nest-matrons also maintain a disposable force of leathanam and Witch Aelves to perform lesser roles upon the battlefield.

ABILITIES

Khaine's Essence: *The drops of divinity that Zainthar Kai warriors carry in their cursed blood elevate them above other Scáthborn.*

Add 1 to the Bravery characteristic of **Zainthar Kai Melusai** units and **Zainthar Kai Khinerai Harpies** units.

Vault of the First Brood: *The heroes of Zainthar Kai maintain a hallowed vault of treasures gifted to them by Morathi.*

You can choose 1 additional **Hero** in your army to have an artefact of power.

COMMAND ABILITY

Power in the Blood: *Zainthar Kai leaders can awaken the godly might running through the veins of their followers, granting them even greater power.*

You can use this command ability once per phase when you pick a friendly **Zainthar Kai Melusai** unit or a friendly **Zainthar Kai Khinerai Harpies** unit to fight and that unit is wholly within 12" of a friendly **Zainthar Kai Hero**. If you do so, add 1 to the Attacks characteristic of melee weapons used by that unit until the end of the phase.

COMMAND TRAIT

A **Zainthar Kai** general must have this command trait instead of one listed on pages 62-63.

Curse of the Bloody-Handed: *So fiercely do the champions of the Zainthar Kai blaze with the dead god's fury that it can cause their enemies' very blood to boil.*

At the end of the combat phase, roll a dice for each enemy unit within 3" of this general. On a 5+, that unit suffers D3 mortal wounds.

ARTEFACT OF POWER

The first **Zainthar Kai Melusai Hero** to receive an artefact of power must be given the Crimson Talisman.

Crimson Talisman: *One of the treasures of the first brood, a crimson glow emanates from this talisman that protects the bearer from would-be assailants.*

Subtract 1 from wound rolls for attacks made with melee weapons that target the bearer.

BATTLEPLAN

CEREMONY OF BLOOD

The Máthcoir – the great Mother Cauldron and font of Morathi's power – has been terribly damaged. Its cursed iron surface has splintered and must be repaired through rite and sacrifice; without this well of dark sorcery, Hagg Nar will surely be lost. Morathi-Khaine herself leads a great ritual intended to heal the Máthcoir's wounds, channelling a vast quantity of potent gore through a sacred sacrificial shrine magically linked to the Mother Cauldron. But enemies seek to impede her plans; they must be driven back – or fed to the Máthcoir themselves.

This battleplan lets you stage a macabre ritual with your Daughters of Khaine army, even as the enemy seeks to disrupt it.

THE ARMIES

Each player picks an army. One player is the Daughters of Khaine player. Their opponent is the Usurper. The Daughters of Khaine player must use a Daughters of Khaine army that includes Morathi-Khaine and the Shadow Queen.

THE BATTLEFIELD

First, set up 4 Blood Font markers in the locations shown on the map. Then, set up an appropriate terrain feature to represent the Ritual Shrine at the centre of the battlefield.

SET-UP

The Daughters of Khaine player sets up Morathi-Khaine and the Shadow Queen within 1" of the Ritual Shrine. The remaining units in the Daughters of Khaine army must be set up wholly within 6" of any Blood Font markers. The Usurper then sets up their army wholly within their territory, as shown on the map.

FIRST TURN

The Usurper takes the first turn in the first battle round.

COMMAND ABILITY

The following additional command ability can be used in this battle.

We Cannot Fail: *The Usurper knows that they are running out of time and must make a desperate gamble.*

The Usurper can use this command ability at the end of their turn if any units from their army have been destroyed. If they do so, they can roll a dice. On a 4+, they can set up 1 destroyed unit from their army wholly within their territory and more than 3" from any enemy units.

IT MUST BE DESTROYED

The Ritual Shrine is protected against enchantment and magic, but raw, brute force may be enough to shatter it.

Units in the Usurper's army treat the Ritual Shrine in the centre of the battlefield as an enemy model and can attack it with melee weapons (it is not affected by spells or abilities). The Ritual Shrine is considered to have a Wounds characteristic of 12 and a Save characteristic of 5+.

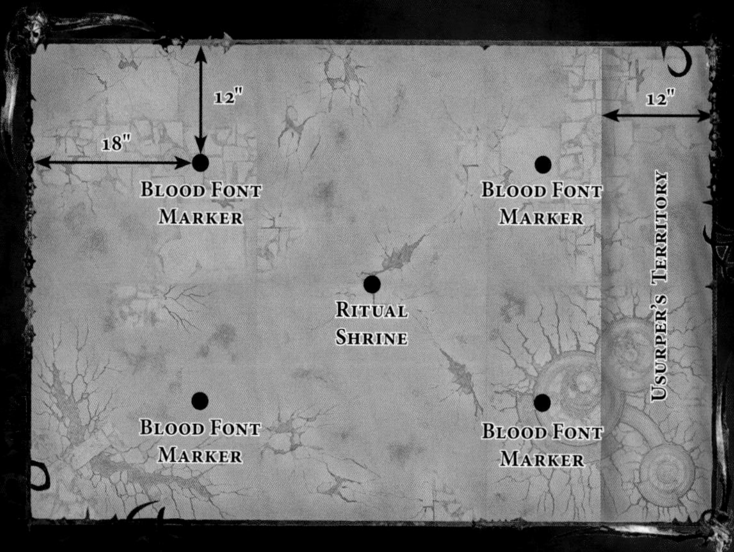

BLOOD FONTS

These sacred fonts are filled with the hot blood of recent sacrifices.

The Blood Font markers in this battle are controlled in the same way as objectives.

At the end of each of their turns, the Daughters of Khaine player can roll a dice for each Blood Font marker that they control. On a 5+, they can heal up to D3 wounds allocated to the Ritual Shrine in the centre of the battlefield.

BATTLE LENGTH

The battle lasts until the Ritual Shrine in the centre of the battlefield is destroyed or for 5 battle rounds, whichever happens first.

GLORIOUS VICTORY

If the Ritual Shrine in the centre of the battlefield is destroyed, the Usurper wins a **major victory**.

If the Ritual Shrine in the centre of the battlefield has fewer than 6 wounds allocated to it at the end of the battle, the Daughters of Khaine player wins a **major victory**.

If neither player has won a **major victory**, the player who controls the most Blood Font markers at the end of the battle wins a **minor victory**.

If both players control the same number of Blood Font markers at the end of the battle, the battle is a **draw**.

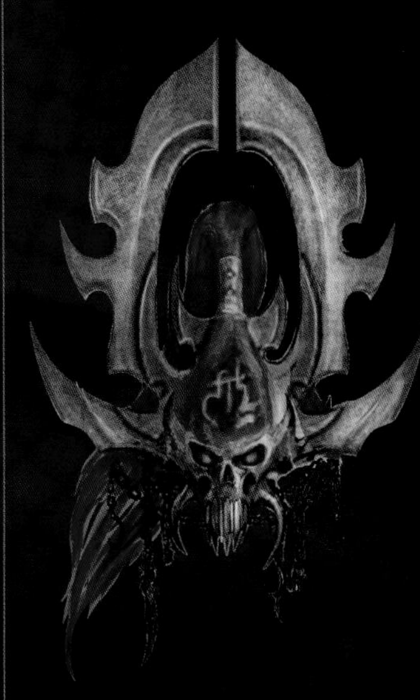

PATH TO GLORY

Path to Glory campaigns centre around collecting and fighting a series of battles in the Mortal Realms. Players start off with a small warband. Over the course of several battles, each warband will gather more followers to join them in their quest for glory and renown.

In order to take part in a Path to Glory campaign, you will need two or more players. Each player will need a **Hero** to be their champion and must then create a warband to follow and fight beside their champion during the campaign.

The players fight battles against each other using the warbands they have created. The results of these battles will gain their warbands glory. After battle, warbands may swell in numbers as more warriors flock to their banner, or existing troops may become more powerful.

After gaining sufficient glory or growing your warband enough to dominate all others through sheer weight of numbers, you will be granted a final test. Succeed, and you will be crowned the victor of the campaign, your glory affirmed for all time.

CREATING A WARBAND

In a Path to Glory game, you do not select your army in the normal manner. Instead, you create a warband that consists of a mighty champion, battling to earn the favour of the gods, and their followers. The details and progress of each warband need to be recorded on a warband roster, which you can download for free from games-workshop.com.

To create a warband, simply follow these steps and record the results on your warband roster:

1. First, pick a faction for your warband. Each faction has its own set of warband tables that are used to generate the units in the warband and the rewards they can receive for fighting battles. The warband tables included in this battletome let you collect a Daughters of Khaine warband, but other Warhammer Age of Sigmar publications include warband tables to let you collect warbands from other factions.

2. Next, choose your warband's champion by selecting one of the options from your faction's champion table. Give your champion a suitably grand name and write this down on your warband roster.

3. Having picked your champion, the next step is to make follower rolls to generate your starting followers. The champion you chose in step 2 will determine how many follower rolls you have. To make a follower roll, pick a column from one of the followers tables and then roll a dice. If you prefer, instead of rolling a dice, you can pick the result from the followers table (this still uses up the roll).

   Sometimes a table will require you to expend two or more rolls, or one roll and a number of Glory Points (see Gaining Glory), in order to use it. Note that the option to expend Glory Points can only be used when you add new followers to your warband after a battle (see Rewards of Battle). In either case, in order to generate a follower unit from the table, you must have enough rolls and/or Glory Points to meet the requirements, and you can then either roll once on the table or pick one result from the table of your choice. If you expend Glory Points, you must reduce your Glory Points total by the amount shown on the table.

   Followers are organised into units. The followers table tells you how many models the unit has. Follower units cannot include additional models, but they can otherwise take any options listed on their warscroll. Record all of the information about your followers on your warband roster.

4. You can use 1 follower roll to allow your champion to start the campaign with a Champion's Reward or to allow 1 of your follower units to start the campaign with a Follower's Reward (see Rewards of Battle).

5. Finally, give your warband a name, one that will inspire respect and dread in your rivals. Your warband is now complete and you can fight your first battle. Good luck!

TO WAR!

Having created a warband, you can now fight battles with it against other warbands taking part in the campaign. You can fight battles as and when you wish, and you can use any of the battleplans available for Warhammer Age of Sigmar. The units you use for a game must be those on your roster.

When you use a Daughters of Khaine warband in a Path to Glory game, you can use all the battle traits from page 61 except the Temples of Khaine battle trait. You cannot use any other Daughters of Khaine allegiance abilities.

Any casualties suffered by a warband are assumed to have been replaced in time for its next battle. If your champion is slain in a battle, it is assumed that they were merely injured; they are back to full strength for your next game, thirsty for vengeance!

GAINING GLORY

All of the players in the campaign are vying for glory. The amount of glory they have received is represented by the Glory Points that the warband has accumulated.

As a warband's glory increases, it will also attract additional followers, and a warband's champion may be granted rewards.

Warbands receive Glory Points after a battle is complete. If the warband drew or lost the battle, it receives 1 Glory Point. If it won the battle, it receives D3 Glory Points (re-roll a result of 1 if it won a **major victory**).

Add the Glory Points you scored to the total recorded on your roster. Once you have won 10 Glory Points, you will have a chance to win the campaign (see Eternal Glory).

REWARDS OF BATTLE

After each battle, you can take one of the three following options. Alternatively, roll a D3 to determine which option to take.

D3	Option
1	**Additional Followers:** *More loyal followers flock to your banner.* You receive 1 follower roll that can be used to select a new unit from a followers table and add it to your warband roster. See step 3 of Creating a Warband for details of how to use the followers table to add a unit to your warband. Once 5 new units have joined your warband, you will have a chance to win the campaign (see Eternal Glory).
2	**Champion's Reward:** *Your champion's prowess grows.* Roll on the champion rewards table for your warband and note the result on your warband roster. Your champion can only receive 1 Champion's Reward – if they already have a Champion's Reward, you must take a Follower's Reward instead.
3	**Follower's Reward:** *Your warriors become renowned for mighty deeds.* Pick 1 unit of followers and then roll on the followers rewards table for your warband. Note the result on your warband roster. A unit can only receive 1 Follower's Reward. If all of your follower units have a Follower's Reward, you must take Additional Followers instead.

ETERNAL GLORY

There are two ways to win a Path to Glory campaign: by Blood or by Might. To win by Blood, your warband must first have 10 Glory Points. To win by Might, your warband must have at least 5 additional units of followers. In either case, you must then fight and win one more battle to win the campaign. If the next battle you fight is tied or lost, you do not receive any Glory Points – just keep on fighting battles until you win the campaign… or another player wins first!

You can shorten or lengthen a campaign by lowering or raising the number of Glory Points needed to win by Blood or the number of extra units that must join a warband to win by Might. For example, for a shorter campaign, you could say that a warband only needs 5 Glory Points before the final fight, or for a longer one, you could say that 15 are needed.

DAUGHTERS OF KHAINE WARBAND TABLES

Use the following tables to determine the champion that leads your warband, the followers that make up the units that fight at their side, and the rewards they receive after battle.

CHAMPION TABLE	
Champion	**Follower Rolls**
Hag Queen on Cauldron of Blood	2
Slaughter Queen on Cauldron of Blood	2
Bloodwrack Shrine	3
Bloodwrack Medusa	4
Melusai Ironscale	4
Hag Queen	5
Slaughter Queen	5

HERO FOLLOWERS TABLE	
D6	**Followers**
1	1 Hag Queen
2-3	1 Slaughter Queen
4-5	1 Bloodwrack Medusa
6	1 Melusai Ironscale

RETINUE FOLLOWERS TABLE	
D6	**Followers**
1	10 Witch Aelves
2	10 Sisters of Slaughter
3	5 Khinerai Heartrenders
4	5 Khinerai Lifetakers
5	5 Blood Sisters
6	5 Blood Stalkers

ELITE RETINUE FOLLOWERS TABLE (uses 2 rolls, or 1 roll and 1 Glory Point)	
D6	**Followers**
1-2	5 Doomfire Warlocks
3	1 Avatar of Khaine
4	1 Bloodwrack Shrine
5	1 Hag Queen on Cauldron of Blood
6	1 Slaughter Queen on Cauldron of Blood

FOLLOWERS REWARDS TABLE

D6 Reward

1 Daughters of Morathi: *These exemplars of faith in the ascended goddess strive to prove their worth when set upon the enemy.*

Add 1 to the number of the current battle round when determining the abilities gained by this unit from the Blood Rites battle trait (pg 61). This ability and other similar abilities are cumulative.

2 Bladed Killers: *These she-aelves are among the most ferocious warriors in the Mortal Realms.*

Improve the Rend characteristic of this unit's melee weapons by 1 if this unit made a charge move in the same turn.

3 Disciples of Slaughter: *These warriors refuse to cease their assault until every last drop of blood in the enemy's veins has been claimed.*

Each time this unit fights for the first time in a phase, after all of its attacks have been resolved, you can roll a dice. On a 6, this unit can fight for a second time, but it cannot fight again in that phase.

4 Concealment and Stealth: *Masked by the banks of mist that follow their warpaths, these warriors are almost impossible to strike at range.*

Subtract 1 from hit rolls for attacks made with missile weapons that target this unit.

5 Strike and Fade: *These followers slice at the enemy with great speed and athleticism, only to retreat again and again until their foe is powerless to resist their fate.*

This unit can retreat and still charge later in the same turn.

6 Khaine's Essence: *The drops of divinity that these warriors carry in their cursed blood elevate them above other followers.*

Add 2 to the Bravery characteristic of this unit.

CHAMPION REWARDS TABLE

D12	Reward
1	**Bathed in Blood:** *This champion bathes in sacrificial blood before battle, rejuvenating her and granting her healing powers.* Add 1 to this champion's Wounds characteristic. In addition, at the start of your hero phase, you can heal 1 wound allocated to this champion.
2	**Zealous Orator:** *This champion is a skilled demagogue whose fiery oratory and utter disdain for weakness inspires her followers to fight on in the face of impossible odds.* Add 2 to the Bravery characteristic of friendly **DAUGHTERS OF KHAINE** units while they are wholly within 12" of this champion.
3	**Sacrificial Overseer:** *This champion has sacrificed countless victims upon the altars of her temple, and she is just as adept at offering lives to Khaine on the battlefield.* Add 1 to hit rolls for attacks made with melee weapons by this champion.
4	**Formidable Visage:** *This champion is possessed of a supernatural form that both captivates and horrifies her foes.* Subtract 1 from hit rolls for attacks made with melee weapons that target this champion.
5	**Master of Poisons:** *This champion has intimate knowledge of all poisons and coats her blades in an elixir that can kill a warrior with the merest scratch.* Add 1 to the damage inflicted by each successful attack made by this champion.
6	**True Believer:** *This champion truly believes that she has been chosen for greatness, a conceit from which she draws great strength.* Add 1 to the number of the current battle round when determining the abilities gained by this champion from the Blood Rites battle trait (pg 61). This ability and other similar abilities are cumulative.
7	**Arcane Proficiency:** *This champion weaves strands of magical energy into perfectly formed spells.* This champion is a **WIZARD** and knows the Arcane Bolt and Mystic Shield spells. They can attempt to cast 1 spell or dispel 1 endless spell in your hero phase and attempt to unbind 1 spell in the enemy hero phase. In addition, you can re-roll 1 casting, dispelling or unbinding roll for this champion. If this champion is already a **WIZARD**, they can attempt to cast 1 extra spell in your hero phase.
8	**Blinding Speed:** *This champion uses cunning movements to confuse and trap her prey.* Subtract 1 from hit rolls for attacks made with missile weapons that target this champion.
9	**Fearsome Presence:** *This champion radiates an aura of ruthless capability.* You can re-roll failed battleshock tests for friendly **DAUGHTERS OF KHAINE** units while they are wholly within 12" of this champion.
10	**Veteran of the Cathtrar Dhule:** *This champion has commanded her forces in the fiercest of battles.* If this champion is part of your army and on the battlefield at the start of your hero phase, roll a dice. On a 4+, you receive 1 extra command point.
11	**Impenetrable Defences:** *Even honed blades find it all but impossible to penetrate this champion's form.* Improve this champion's Save characteristic by 1.
12	**Fuelled by Vengeance:** *This champion inspires a wrathful lust for revenge in her warriors.* Once per battle, in your hero phase, you can use a command ability on this champion's warscroll without spending any command points. If this champion does not have a command ability, re-roll this result.

WARSCROLLS

WARSCROLL BATTALION

WAR COVEN OF MORATHI

No longer does Morathi attempt to rule through whispers and manipulation alone. Instead, she marches to battle at the fore of her own war coven, eager to smite any who defy her will. Those who dare oppose the Daughters of Khaine find they must pay a steep price in their own blood.

ORGANISATION

- 1 Vyperic Guard
- 1 Cauldron Guard
- 1 Slaughter Troupe
- 1 Scáthcoven
- 1 Shadow Patrol

ABILITIES

Devout Followers: *The faithful of Morathi are fearless in their actions when under the gaze of their goddess.*

Do not take battleshock tests for units from this battalion if **MORATHI-KHAINE** is part of your army and on the battlefield.

This section includes Daughters of Khaine warscrolls, warscroll battalions, and endless spell and invocation of Khaine warscrolls. Updated February 2021; the warscrolls printed here take precedence over any warscrolls with an earlier publication date or no publication date.

The painted orruk howled and swung its club. Sziatha bent her back and let the weapon whip over her head before darting forward with a quick cross-slice that opened her foe's throat.

She twirled, exulting in the sensation of gore splattering across her skin.

'Blood for Khaine!' she screamed.

Through a crimson mask, Sziatha saw the Axenhall militia – the Khainites' supposed allies – struggling to hold back the orruks, slipping and sliding in the brackish mud as the greenskins' greater strength drove them back. What clumsy oafs they were.

She came in lightning fast, hearing the howls of her sisters at her side. They leapt at the rear of the orruks' line, stabbing down with their twin daggers like the claws of a cave-mantis. The slaughter commenced.

Sziatha's world became one of steel and red and splintered bone as she pirouetted amidst the carnage.

The Witch Aelf's blades screeched across something hard and smooth. Momentary confusion dragged her from her reverie. Orruks did not wear metal.

Her red vision cleared, and she saw that she was looking into the surprised face of a sandy-haired militiaman. Her sciansá had skipped off his breastplate and sliced a wide smile across his throat. He seemed more surprised than accusing as he looked into the face of his supposed rescuer. His hot blood sprayed across Sziatha's face. Then his eyes rolled back, and he toppled to the muddy earth.

Sziatha did not even spare the man's twitching body a second thought. She was already racing off in pursuit of her next kill.

WARSCROLL BATTALION

CAULDRON GUARD

ORGANISATION

- 1 **Hag Queen**
- 2 units of Witch Aelves
- 2 units of Khinerai Lifetakers

ABILITIES

Frenzied Devotees: *The Cauldron Guard seek to carve a path for their worshipped engines through enemy defences at the earliest opportunity.*

Add 1 to run and charge rolls for units from this battalion.

WARSCROLL BATTALION

SLAUGHTER TROUPE

ORGANISATION

- 1 **Slaughter Queen**
- 2 units of Sisters of Slaughter
- 2 units of Khinerai Heartrenders

ABILITIES

Gladiatorial Acrobatics: *The warriors of a Slaughter Troupe are almost impossible to catch in the heat of battle.*

Units from this battalion can retreat and still shoot and/or charge later in the same turn.

WARSCROLL BATTALION

SHADOW PATROL

ORGANISATION

- 2 units of Doomfire Warlocks
- 4 units of **Khinerai Harpies**

ABILITIES

Shadowpaths: *Shadow Patrols can travel via the shadows themselves, covering vast distances in the blink of an eye. Nowhere is safe from these warriors.*

In your movement phase, instead of making a normal move with a unit from this battalion, you can say that it will navigate the shadowpaths. If you do so, remove that unit from the battlefield and set it up again anywhere on the battlefield more than 9" from any enemy units.

WARSCROLL BATTALION

SCÁTHCOVEN

ORGANISATION

- 1 **Bloodwrack Medusa** or Melusai Ironscale
- 1-4 units of Blood Sisters
- 1-2 units of Blood Stalkers
- 0-2 units of **Khinerai Harpies**

ABILITIES

Devoted to Morathi: *The warriors of a Scáthcoven are utterly dedicated to Morathi's cause, and they will fight without fear of pain or death in order to carry out her will.*

Do not take battleshock tests for units from this battalion.

WARSCROLL BATTALION

VYPERIC GUARD

ORGANISATION

- Morathi-Khaine
- The Shadow Queen
- 1-2 Bloodwrack Medusae or Melusai Ironscales in any combination
- 2-3 units of Blood Sisters or Blood Stalkers in any combination

ABILITIES

Vaunted Slayers: *The Melusai that make up Morathi's famed Vyperic Guard are unwaveringly loyal and the finest warriors of their kind.*

Once per battle, a **Hero** from this battalion can use a command ability without a command point being spent.

WARSCROLL BATTALION

SHRINE BROOD

ORGANISATION

- 2 Bloodwrack Shrines
- 2 units of Blood Sisters or Blood Stalkers in any combination
- 2 units of **Khinerai Harpies**

ABILITIES

Blood Sacrifice: *The warriors of a Shrine Brood will sacrifice their own lives in order to revitalise the Bloodwrack Shrine they are sworn to protect.*

In your hero phase, you can pick any number of units from this battalion that are within 6" of the **Bloodwrack Shrine** from the same battalion. 1 model from each unit you picked is slain. You can heal 1 wound allocated to the **Bloodwrack Shrine** for each **Khinerai Harpies** model that was slain, and you can heal up to 2 wounds allocated to the **Bloodwrack Shrine** for each **Melusai** model that was slain.

• WARSCROLL •

MORATHI-KHAINE

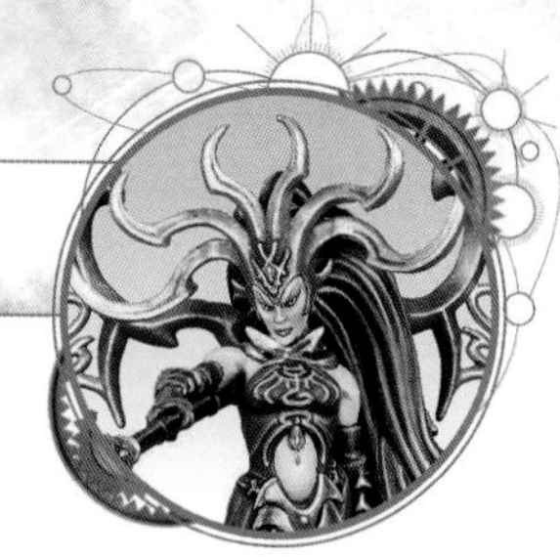

Proclaiming herself Khaine reborn, the goddess Morathi bestrides the realms, summoning snaking tendrils of shadow magic to tear apart her enemies. She is a master of manipulation and deception, endlessly cunning and depthlessly cruel.

MELEE WEAPONS	Range	Attacks	To Hit	To Wound	Rend	Damage
Heartrender	2"	3	3+	3+	-1	D3
Bladed Wings	2"	6	3+	3+	-1	1

DESCRIPTION

Morathi-Khaine is a named character that is a single model. She is armed with Heartrender and Bladed Wings.

If this model is included in a Daughters of Khaine army, this model is treated as a general in addition to the model that is chosen to be the army general.

THE SHADOW QUEEN: If this model is included in an army, then the army must include the Shadow Queen. References to the Shadow Queen on this warscroll refer to the Shadow Queen model in the same army as this model.

ABILITIES

Commanding Presence: *Very few foes are able to resist quailing before Morathi's regal presence.*

Subtract 1 from hit rolls for attacks that target this model.

One Soul, Two Bodies: *Morathi-Khaine and the Shadow Queen are two entities but share the same life force.*

If the Shadow Queen is on the battlefield, wounds and mortal wounds that would be allocated to this model are instead allocated to the Shadow Queen and have no effect on this model. Wounds and mortal wounds allocated to the Shadow Queen in this way cannot be negated.

In addition, if the Shadow Queen is on the battlefield and an ability or spell would cause this model to be slain without any wounds being allocated, then this model is not slain and 3 wounds are allocated to the Shadow Queen.

If the Shadow Queen is slain, after her model is removed from play, this model is also slain.

MAGIC

This model is a **WIZARD**. It can attempt to cast 3 spells in your hero phase and attempt to unbind 2 spells in the enemy hero phase. Add 1 to casting, dispelling and unbinding rolls for this model.

This model knows the Arcane Bolt, Mystic Shield and Black Horror of Ulgu spells.

Black Horror of Ulgu: *A roiling black cloud of energy swirls into existence, smoking tendrils lashing out from it to drag those nearby to their doom.*

Black Horror of Ulgu has a casting value of 7 and a range of 36". If successfully cast, pick 1 enemy unit within range of the caster that is visible to them and roll a dice. On a 1, that unit suffers 1 mortal wound. On a 2-3, it suffers D3 mortal wounds. On a 4+, it suffers D6 mortal wounds.

COMMAND ABILITY

Worship Through Bloodshed: *At Morathi's command, her warriors launch into a killing frenzy that sees their foes slain in droves.*

If this model is on the battlefield, you can use this command ability in your hero phase. If you do, pick 1 other friendly **DAUGHTERS OF KHAINE** unit wholly within 24" of this model. That unit can shoot or, if it is within 3" of any enemy units, it can fight. You cannot use this command ability more than once in the same phase.

KEYWORDS	ORDER, AELF, DAUGHTERS OF KHAINE, HERO, WIZARD, MORATHI-KHAINE

• WARSCROLL •

THE SHADOW QUEEN

The Shadow Queen is Morathi-Khaine's dark reflection, the accumulation of all her hatred and bitterness given monstrous, serpentine form. Those who would challenge this nightmare in battle are soon slain in a blur of shadowsteel and lashing coils.

MISSILE WEAPONS	Range	Attacks	To Hit	To Wound	Rend	Damage
Gaze of the Shadow Queen	18"	1	2+	2+	-3	D6
MELEE WEAPONS	**Range**	**Attacks**	**To Hit**	**To Wound**	**Rend**	**Damage**
Heartrender	2"	✹	3+	3+	-1	3
Crown of Serpents	1"	2D6	3+	3+	-	1
Envenomed Tail	3"	1	3+	3+	-2	✹

DAMAGE TABLE			
Wounds Suffered	**Move**	**Heartrender**	**Envenomed Tail**
0-3	14"	8	6
4-6	12"	7	5
7-8	10"	6	4
9-10	8"	5	3
11+	6"	4	2

DESCRIPTION

The Shadow Queen is a named character that is a single model. She is armed with Gaze of the Shadow Queen, Heartrender, Crown of Serpents and Envenomed Tail.

This model cannot be a general.

MORATHI-KHAINE: If this model is included in an army, then the army must include Morathi-Khaine. References to Morathi-Khaine on this warscroll refer to the Morathi-Khaine model in the same army as this model.

FLY: This model can fly.

ABILITIES

Fury of the Shadow Queen: *Bloodshed raises the Shadow Queen's fury to new heights, in turn fuelling the murderlust of nearby Scáthborn.*

While this model is within 3" of any enemy models, add 1 to the Attacks characteristic of melee weapons used by friendly **Khinerai Harpies** and **Melusai** units wholly within 18" of this model.

Two Bodies, One Soul: *The Shadow Queen and Morathi-Khaine are two entities but share the same life force.*

If this model is on the battlefield, wounds and mortal wounds that would be allocated to Morathi-Khaine are instead allocated to this model and have no effect on Morathi-Khaine. Wounds and mortal wounds allocated to this model in this way cannot be negated.

In addition, if this model is on the battlefield and an ability or spell would cause Morathi-Khaine to be slain without any wounds being allocated, then Morathi-Khaine is not slain and 3 wounds are allocated to this model.

If this model is slain, after this model is removed from play, Morathi-Khaine is also slain.

Iron Heart of Khaine: *The Iron Heart of Khaine is the last remnant of the fallen god, and it pulses still with life-sustaining divine energies.*

No more than 3 wounds and/or mortal wounds can be suffered by this model in the same turn. Once 3 wounds and/or mortal wounds have been allocated to this model in the same turn, not counting any wounds that were negated, any further wounds and mortal wounds that would be allocated to this model are ignored and have no effect.

Wounds and mortal wounds allocated to this model at the start of the battle round count towards the number of wounds allocated to this model in the first turn of that battle round. Wounds and mortal wounds allocated to this model at the end of the battle round count towards the number of wounds allocated to this model in the second turn of that battle round.

If the rule for an ability or spell would cause this model to be slain without any wounds being allocated, 3 wounds are allocated to this model instead. These wounds cannot be negated but will still be ignored once 3 wounds and/or mortal wounds have been allocated to this model.

Wounds allocated to this model cannot be healed.

KEYWORDS	ORDER, AELF, DAUGHTERS OF KHAINE, MONSTER, HERO, THE SHADOW QUEEN

• WARSCROLL •

BLOODWRACK SHRINE

Doom spreads from the Bloodwrack Shrine, waves of agonising pain pouring out as the altar ploughs forward. Hissing, the Bloodwrack Medusa that slithers atop the shrine unleashes spells of malevolence while casting her deathly stare across the battlefield.

MISSILE WEAPONS	Range	Attacks	To Hit	To Wound	Rend	Damage
Bloodwrack Stare	12"	See below				
MELEE WEAPONS	**Range**	**Attacks**	**To Hit**	**To Wound**	**Rend**	**Damage**
Bloodwrack Spear	2"	3	3+	3+	-1	D3
Goadstaves	2"	✸	3+	3+	-	1
Whisperclaw	1"	4	4+	3+	-	1
Tail of Serpents	2"	D6	4+	4+	-	1

DAMAGE TABLE			
Wounds Suffered	**Move**	**Goadstaves**	**Aura of Agony**
0-3	6"	6	2+
4-6	5"	5	3+
7-10	4"	4	4+
11+	3"	3	5+

DESCRIPTION

A Bloodwrack Shrine is a single model armed with a Bloodwrack Stare, Bloodwrack Spear, Goadstaves, Whisperclaw and Tail of Serpents.

ABILITIES

Aura of Agony: *Bloodwrack Shrines emit an aura that causes waves of agony to course through the enemy.*

At the start of your hero phase, you can roll 1 dice for each enemy unit within 7" of this model. If the roll is equal to or greater than the Aura of Agony value shown on this model's damage table, that unit suffers D3 mortal wounds. The same unit cannot be affected by this ability more than once per turn.

Bladed Impact: *The bladed carriage of a Bloodwrack Shrine can cleave its way through enemy ranks with ease.*

After this model makes a charge move, you can pick 1 enemy unit within 1" of this model and roll a dice. On a 2+, that enemy unit suffers D3 mortal wounds.

Bloodwrack Stare: *Should a victim's eyes lock with a Bloodwrack Medusa's stare for even a second, their life blood will violently rebel, flooding from every pore until their body collapses into a pool of gore.*

Do not use the attack sequence for an attack made with this model's Bloodwrack Stare. Instead, roll a number of dice equal to the number of models from the target unit that are in range of the attack. For each 5+, the target unit suffers 1 mortal wound.

Whisperclaw: *This razor-edged talon can carve through any resistance it meets.*

If the unmodified hit roll for an attack made with a Whisperclaw is 6, that attack inflicts 1 mortal wound on the target and the attack sequence ends (do not make a wound or save roll).

MAGIC

This model is a **WIZARD**. It can attempt to cast 1 spell in your hero phase and attempt to unbind 2 spells in the enemy hero phase. It knows the Arcane Bolt, Mystic Shield and Enfeebling Foe spells.

Enfeebling Foe: *The Bloodwrack Medusa reaches into her victims' minds, sapping their strength.*

Enfeebling Foe has a casting value of 5. If successfully cast, pick 1 enemy unit within 18" of the caster that is visible to them. Subtract 1 from wound rolls for attacks made with melee weapons by that unit until your next hero phase.

KEYWORDS	ORDER, AELF, DAUGHTERS OF KHAINE, MELUSAI, HERO, WIZARD, TOTEM, BLOODWRACK MEDUSA, BLOODWRACK SHRINE

• WARSCROLL •

BLOODWRACK MEDUSA

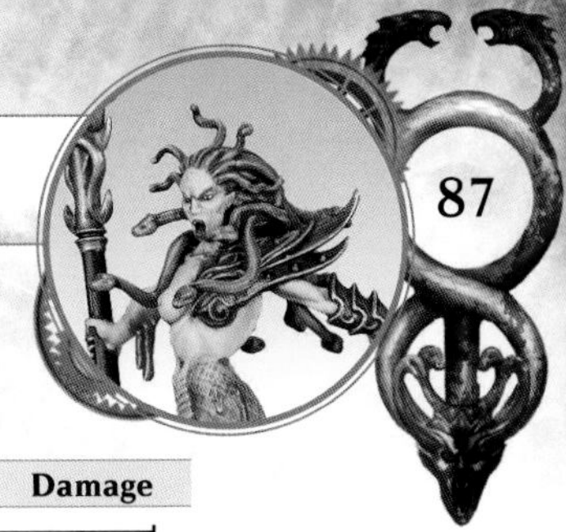

Bloodwrack Medusae are sorceresses gifted – or cursed – with enormous serpentine bodies and heads crowned with snakes. They are so full of spite and shadow magic that to meet their horrific gaze can cause explosive haemorrhaging.

MISSILE WEAPONS	Range	Attacks	To Hit	To Wound	Rend	Damage
Bloodwrack Stare	12"	See below				
MELEE WEAPONS	**Range**	**Attacks**	**To Hit**	**To Wound**	**Rend**	**Damage**
Bloodwrack Spear	2"	3	3+	3+	-1	D3
Whisperclaw	1"	4	4+	3+	-	1
Tail of Serpents	2"	D6	4+	4+	-	1

DESCRIPTION

A Bloodwrack Medusa is a single model armed with a Bloodwrack Stare, Bloodwrack Spear, Whisperclaw and Tail of Serpents.

ABILITIES

Bloodwrack Stare: *Should a victim's eyes lock with a Bloodwrack Medusa's stare for even a second, their life blood will violently rebel, flooding from every pore until their body collapses into a pool of gore.*

Do not use the attack sequence for an attack made with this model's Bloodwrack Stare. Instead, roll a number of dice equal to the number of models from the target unit that are in range of the attack. For each 5+, the target unit suffers 1 mortal wound.

Whisperclaw: *This razor-edged talon can carve through any resistance it meets.*

If the unmodified hit roll for an attack made with a Whisperclaw is 6, that attack inflicts 1 mortal wound on the target and the attack sequence ends (do not make a wound or save roll).

MAGIC

This model is a **WIZARD**. It can attempt to cast 1 spell in your hero phase and attempt to unbind 2 spells in the enemy hero phase. It knows the Arcane Bolt, Mystic Shield and Enfeebling Foe spells.

Enfeebling Foe: *The Bloodwrack Medusa reaches into her victims' minds, sapping their strength.*

Enfeebling Foe has a casting value of 5. If successfully cast, pick 1 enemy unit within 18" of the caster that is visible to them. Subtract 1 from wound rolls for attacks made with melee weapons by that unit until your next hero phase.

KEYWORDS	ORDER, DAUGHTERS OF KHAINE, MELUSAI, HERO, WIZARD, BLOODWRACK MEDUSA

• WARSCROLL •

MELUSAI IRONSCALE

Crafted from the souls of aelves that blazed brightest with the need for revenge, the Melusai Ironscales serve Morathi as elite war leaders amongst the Scáthborn and are terrifying martial champions in their own right.

MISSILE WEAPONS	Range	Attacks	To Hit	To Wound	Rend	Damage
Keldrisaíth	18"	3	3+	3+	-1	1
MELEE WEAPONS	**Range**	**Attacks**	**To Hit**	**To Wound**	**Rend**	**Damage**
Keldrisaíth	2"	3	3+	3+	-1	D3

DESCRIPTION

A Melusai Ironscale is a single model armed with a Keldrisaíth.

ABILITIES

Blood of the Oracle: *The soul of each Melusai Ironscale has been specially experimented upon by Morathi to increase their resistance to hostile magics.*

Each time this model is affected by a spell or endless spell, you can roll a dice. If you do so, on a 5+, ignore the effects of that spell or endless spell on this model.

Gory Offering: *As a Melusai Ironscale holds the crystallised heart of a slain foe aloft, the power of Khaine pulses through it, empowering any fellow Melusai nearby.*

If any enemy models are slain by wounds inflicted by this model's attacks in the combat phase, you can add 1 to the Attacks characteristic of friendly **Melusai** units wholly within 12" of this model until the end of that phase.

Turned to Crystal: *The scáth touch of a Melusai Ironscale can permanently transmute an enemy into an immobile – though still fully conscious – crystal statue.*

At the end of the combat phase, you can pick 1 enemy unit within 1" of this model and roll a dice. On a 3+, that enemy unit suffers 1 mortal wound.

COMMAND ABILITY

Wrath of the Scáthborn: *With a shrieked prayer to Khaine and Morathi, an Ironscale leads her Melusai kin in the swift slaughter of the foe.*

You can use this command ability once per turn in your hero phase. If you do so, pick 1 friendly **Melusai** unit wholly within 12" of this model. Until your next hero phase, that unit can run and still shoot and/or charge later in the same turn. In addition, until your next hero phase, you can roll 2D6 instead of D6 when you make a run roll for that unit.

KEYWORDS	ORDER, DAUGHTERS OF KHAINE, MELUSAI, HERO, MELUSAI IRONSCALE

• WARSCROLL •

MORGWAETH THE BLOODIED

Few of Khaine's bloody-minded worshippers have spilled so much gore in service of their deity than the Hag Queen Morgwaeth, whose blades have opened throats by the thousand and whose fury has seen cities drowned in slaughter.

MELEE WEAPONS	Range	Attacks	To Hit	To Wound	Rend	Damage
Glaive of Khaine	2"	3	3+	3+	-1	1

DESCRIPTION

Morgwaeth the Bloodied is a named character that is a single model. She is armed with a Glaive of Khaine.

ABILITIES

Priestess of Khaine: *In battle, Hag Queens enact blood rites that fill their warriors with a frenzied murderlust.*

In your hero phase, this model can chant 1 of the following prayers. If it does so, pick 1 of the prayers and then make a prayer roll by rolling a dice. On a 1, this model suffers 1 mortal wound and the prayer is not answered. On a 2, the prayer is not answered. On a 3+, the prayer is answered.

Rune of Khaine: If this prayer is answered, until your next hero phase, this model's melee weapon has a Damage characteristic of D3 instead of 1.

Touch of Death: If this prayer is answered, pick 1 enemy unit within 3" of this model. Then, take a dice and hide it in one of your hands. Your opponent must pick one of your hands. If they pick the one holding the dice, that enemy unit suffers D3 mortal wounds.

Witchbrew: *Witchbrew drives the imbiber into such an ecstasy of destruction that they will fight on in the face of impossible odds.*

At the start of your hero phase, you can pick 1 friendly DAUGHTERS OF KHAINE unit wholly within 12" of this model to drink witchbrew. If you do so, roll a dice, adding 1 to the roll for each of the following abilities that this model has gained:

- Headlong Fury
- Zealot's Rage
- Slaughterer's Strength

On a 5+, you can re-roll wound rolls for attacks made with melee weapons by that unit until your next hero phase. In addition, on a 5+, do not take battleshock tests for that unit until your next hero phase.

KEYWORDS ORDER, AELF, DAUGHTERS OF KHAINE, HAGG NAR, HERO, PRIEST, HAG QUEEN, MORGWAETH THE BLOODIED

• WARSCROLL •

THE BLADE-COVEN

A gathering of fearsome zealots follow Hag Queen Morgwaeth on her holy quest to slake the Lord of Murder's bloodthirst, exulting in every slit throat and impaled heart they inflict along the way.

MISSILE WEAPONS	Range	Attacks	To Hit	To Wound	Rend	Damage
Heartseeker Bow	24"	2	3+	3+	-1	1
MELEE WEAPONS	**Range**	**Attacks**	**To Hit**	**To Wound**	**Rend**	**Damage**
Sacrificial Weapons	1"	3	3+	4+	-	1

DESCRIPTION

The Blade-coven is a unit that has 4 models. Kyrae is armed with a Heartseeker Bow and Sacrificial Weapons; and Khamyss, Kyrssa and Lethyr are each armed with Sacrificial Weapons.

KYRAE: Kyrae has a Wounds characteristic of 2.

ABILITIES

Heartseekers: *The blood-blessed arrows loosed by these Melusai unerringly seek out the enemy's vital organs.*

If the unmodified hit roll for an attack made with a Heartseeker Bow is 6, that attack inflicts 1 mortal wound on the target and the attack sequence ends (do not make a wound or save roll).

Zealots of the First Temple: *The Blade-coven are fanatical in their devotion to Hagg Nar and to Morgwaeth.*

Roll a dice before you allocate a wound or mortal wound to a friendly MORGWAETH THE BLOODIED while she is within 3" of this unit. On a 2+, that wound or mortal wound is allocated to this unit instead of MORGWAETH THE BLOODIED.

KEYWORDS ORDER, AELF, MELUSAI, DAUGHTERS OF KHAINE, HAGG NAR, THE BLADE-COVEN

• WARSCROLL •

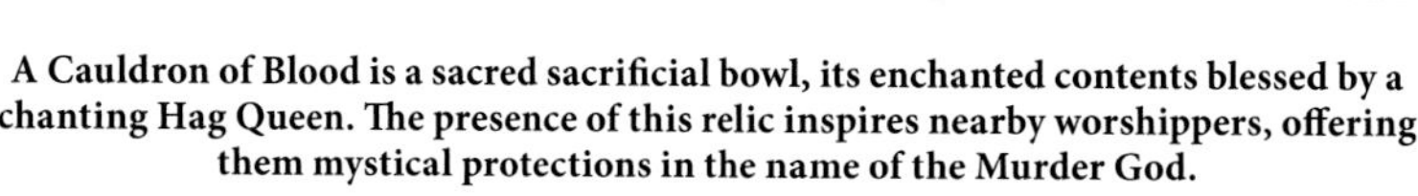

HAG QUEEN

ON CAULDRON OF BLOOD

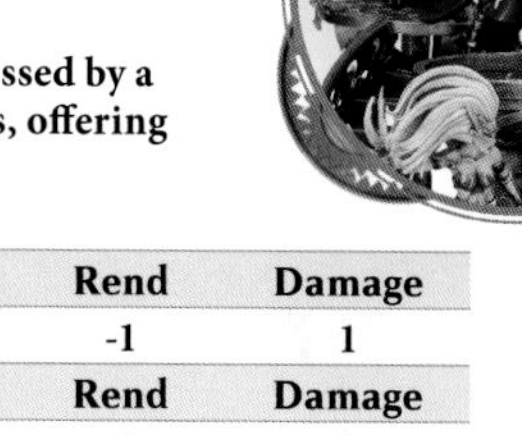

A Cauldron of Blood is a sacred sacrificial bowl, its enchanted contents blessed by a chanting Hag Queen. The presence of this relic inspires nearby worshippers, offering them mystical protections in the name of the Murder God.

MISSILE WEAPONS	Range	Attacks	To Hit	To Wound	Rend	Damage
Torrent of Burning Blood	10"	6	3+	3+	-1	1
MELEE WEAPONS	**Range**	**Attacks**	**To Hit**	**To Wound**	**Rend**	**Damage**
Avatar's Sword	2"	4	3+	3+	-2	3
Blade of Khaine	1"	4	3+	3+	-1	1
Sacrificial Knives	1"	✹	3+	4+	-	1

DAMAGE TABLE			
Wounds Suffered	**Move**	**Sacrificial Knives**	**Bloodshield**
0-3	6"	8	18"
4-6	5"	7	14"
7-9	4"	6	10"
10+	3"	5	6"

DESCRIPTION

A Hag Queen on Cauldron of Blood is a single model armed with a Torrent of Burning Blood, Avatar's Sword, Blade of Khaine and Sacrificial Knives.

ABILITIES

Bladed Impact: *The bladed carriage of a Cauldron of Blood can cleave its way through enemy ranks with ease.*

After this model makes a charge move, you can pick 1 enemy unit within 1" of this model and roll a dice. On a 2+, that enemy unit suffers D3 mortal wounds.

Bloodshield: *The powerful magic that fuels the Cauldron of Blood grants it and nearby followers protection.*

Add 1 to save rolls for attacks that target friendly **Daughters of Khaine** units while they are wholly within the range of any friendly models with this ability. The range of this model's Bloodshield ability is shown on its damage table.

Idol of Worship: *Avatars of Khaine inspire the warrior cults of the Murder God to unleash their relentless potential.*

Add 1 to the Bravery characteristic of friendly **Daughters of Khaine** units while they are wholly within 12" of any friendly models with this ability.

Priestess of Khaine: *Bloodshed and sacrifice calls the might of the Murder God to the battlefield.*

In your hero phase, this model can chant 1 of the following prayers. If it does so, pick 1 of the prayers and make a prayer roll by rolling a dice. On a 1, this model suffers 1 mortal wound and the prayer is not answered. On a 2, the prayer is not answered. On a 3+, the prayer is answered.

Rune of Khaine: If this prayer is answered, until your next hero phase, this model's Blade of Khaine has a Damage characteristic of D3 instead of 1.

Touch of Death: If this prayer is answered, pick 1 enemy unit within 3" of this model. Then, take a dice and hide it in one of your hands. Your opponent must pick one of your hands. If they pick the one holding the dice, that enemy unit suffers D3 mortal wounds.

Wrath of Khaine: *Khaine's subjects channel their faith through bladed idols of the Murder God.*

If your army includes any **Avatars of Khaine**, friendly **Daughters of Khaine Priests** can chant the following prayer.

Animated: Pick 1 friendly **Avatar of Khaine** on the battlefield. Until your next hero phase, that **Avatar of Khaine** is animated.

This model cannot attack with its Torrent of Burning Blood or Avatar's Sword unless its **Avatar of Khaine** is animated.

Witchbrew: *Distilled from the blood of Slaughter Queens, witchbrew drives the imbiber into such an ecstasy of destruction that they will fight on in the face of impossible odds.*

At the start of your hero phase, you can pick 1 friendly **Daughters of Khaine** unit wholly within 12" of this model to drink witchbrew. If you do so, roll a dice, adding 1 to the roll for each of the following abilities that this model has gained:

- Headlong Fury
- Zealot's Rage
- Slaughterer's Strength

On a 5+, you can re-roll wound rolls for attacks made with melee weapons by that unit until your next hero phase. In addition, on a 5+, do not take battleshock tests for that unit until your next hero phase.

KEYWORDS	ORDER, AELF, DAUGHTERS OF KHAINE, HERO, PRIEST, TOTEM, WITCH AELVES, HAG QUEEN, AVATAR OF KHAINE, CAULDRON OF BLOOD

• WARSCROLL •

HAG QUEEN

A Hag Queen is a priestess of Khaine, learned in blood rituals and murder rites. Her curses bring death, and her draughts of witchbrew can stoke the fury of nearby Khainites, driving them to new, feverish heights of violence.

MELEE WEAPONS	Range	Attacks	To Hit	To Wound	Rend	Damage
Blade of Khaine	1"	4	3+	3+	-1	1

DESCRIPTION

A Hag Queen is a single model armed with a Blade of Khaine.

ABILITIES

Priestess of Khaine: *Bloodshed and sacrifice calls the might of the Murder God to the battlefield.*

In your hero phase, this model can chant 1 of the following prayers. If it does so, pick 1 of the prayers and make a prayer roll by rolling a dice. On a 1, this model suffers 1 mortal wound and the prayer is not answered. On a 2, the prayer is not answered. On a 3+, the prayer is answered.

Rune of Khaine: If this prayer is answered, until your next hero phase, this model's Blade of Khaine has a Damage characteristic of D3 instead of 1.

Touch of Death: If this prayer is answered, pick 1 enemy unit within 3" of this model. Then, take a dice and hide it in one of your hands. Your opponent must pick one of your hands. If they pick the one holding the dice, that enemy unit suffers D3 mortal wounds.

Witchbrew: *Distilled from the blood of Slaughter Queens, witchbrew drives the imbiber into such an ecstasy of destruction that they will fight on in the face of impossible odds.*

At the start of your hero phase, you can pick 1 friendly **Daughters of Khaine** unit wholly within 12" of this model to drink witchbrew. If you do so, roll a dice, adding 1 to the roll for each of the following abilities that this model has gained:

- Headlong Fury
- Zealot's Rage
- Slaughterer's Strength

On a 5+, you can re-roll wound rolls for attacks made with melee weapons by that unit until your next hero phase. In addition, on a 5+, do not take battleshock tests for that unit until your next hero phase.

KEYWORDS ORDER, AELF, DAUGHTERS OF KHAINE, HERO, PRIEST, HAG QUEEN

• WARSCROLL •

SLAUGHTER QUEEN

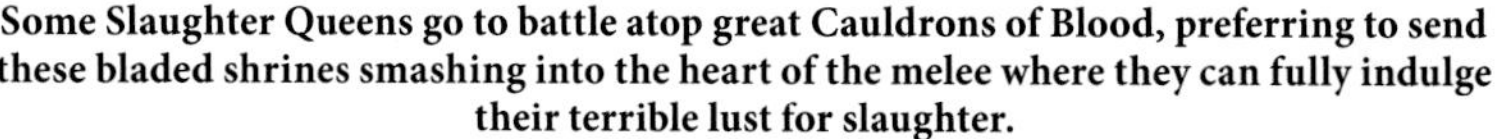

ON CAULDRON OF BLOOD

Some Slaughter Queens go to battle atop great Cauldrons of Blood, preferring to send these bladed shrines smashing into the heart of the melee where they can fully indulge their terrible lust for slaughter.

MISSILE WEAPONS	Range	Attacks	To Hit	To Wound	Rend	Damage
Torrent of Burning Blood	10"	6	3+	3+	-1	1
MELEE WEAPONS	**Range**	**Attacks**	**To Hit**	**To Wound**	**Rend**	**Damage**
Avatar's Sword	2"	4	3+	3+	-2	3
Deathsword	1"	3	3+	3+	-1	D3
Blade of Khaine	1"	4	3+	4+	-1	1
Sacrificial Knives	1"	✹	3+	4+	-	1

DAMAGE TABLE			
Wounds Suffered	**Move**	**Sacrificial Knives**	**Bloodshield**
0-3	6"	8	18"
4-6	5"	7	14"
7-9	4"	6	10"
10+	3"	5	6"

DESCRIPTION

A Slaughter Queen on Cauldron of Blood is a single model armed with a Torrent of Burning Blood, Avatar's Sword, Deathsword, Blade of Khaine and Sacrificial Knives.

ABILITIES

Bladed Impact: *The bladed carriage of a Cauldron of Blood can cleave its way through enemy ranks with ease.*

After this model makes a charge move, you can pick 1 enemy unit within 1" of this model and roll a dice. On a 2+, that enemy unit suffers D3 mortal wounds.

Bloodshield: *The powerful magic that fuels the Cauldron of Blood grants it and nearby followers protection.*

The range of this model's Bloodshield ability is shown on its damage table. Add 1 to save rolls for attacks that target friendly DAUGHTERS OF KHAINE units while they are wholly within the range of any friendly models with this ability.

Idol of Worship: *Avatars of Khaine inspire the warrior cults of the Murder God to unleash their relentless potential.*

Add 1 to the Bravery characteristic of friendly DAUGHTERS OF KHAINE units while they are wholly within 12" of any friendly models with this ability.

Pact of Blood: *Blood oaths to the Murder God protect his subjects from malevolent sorcery.*

This model can attempt to unbind 1 spell in the enemy hero phase in the same manner as a WIZARD.

Priestess of Khaine: *Bloodshed and sacrifice calls the might of the Murder God to the battlefield.*

In your hero phase, this model can chant 1 of the following prayers. If it does so, pick 1 of the prayers and make a prayer roll by rolling a dice. On a 1, this model suffers 1 mortal wound and the prayer is not answered. On a 2, the prayer is not answered. On a 3+, the prayer is answered.

Rune of Khaine: If this prayer is answered, until your next hero phase, this model's Blade of Khaine has a Damage characteristic of D3 instead of 1.

Touch of Death: If this prayer is answered, pick 1 enemy unit within 3" of this model. Then, take a dice and hide it in one of your hands. Your opponent must pick one of your hands. If they pick the one holding the dice, that enemy unit suffers D3 mortal wounds.

Wrath of Khaine: *Khaine's subjects channel their faith through bladed idols of the Murder God.*

If your army includes any AVATARS OF KHAINE, friendly DAUGHTERS OF KHAINE PRIESTS can chant the following prayer.

Animated: Pick 1 friendly AVATAR OF KHAINE on the battlefield. Until your next hero phase, that AVATAR OF KHAINE is animated.

This model cannot attack with its Torrent of Burning Blood or Avatar's Sword unless its AVATAR OF KHAINE is animated.

COMMAND ABILITY

Orgy of Slaughter: *The Slaughter Queen orders her warriors to renew their assault twice over.*

You can use this command ability once per turn in your hero phase. If you do so, pick 1 friendly DAUGHTERS OF KHAINE unit that has not fought in that phase and is wholly within 12" of this model and within 3" of any enemy units. That unit can fight.

KEYWORDS	ORDER, AELF, DAUGHTERS OF KHAINE, HERO, PRIEST, TOTEM, WITCH AELVES, SLAUGHTER QUEEN, AVATAR OF KHAINE, CAULDRON OF BLOOD

• WARSCROLL •

SLAUGHTER QUEEN

It is a Slaughter Queen's role to embody the aggressive martial prowess of Khaine himself. With a blade in each hand, the Slaughter Queen hacks and spins in the maelstrom of close combat while chanting blood-curdling battle rites.

MELEE WEAPONS	Range	Attacks	To Hit	To Wound	Rend	Damage
Deathsword	1"	3	3+	3+	-1	D3
Blade of Khaine	1"	4	3+	4+	-1	1

DESCRIPTION

A Slaughter Queen is a single model armed with a Deathsword and Blade of Khaine.

ABILITIES

Priestess of Khaine: *Bloodshed and sacrifice calls the might of the Murder God to the battlefield.*

In your hero phase, this model can chant 1 of the following prayers. If it does so, pick 1 of the prayers and make a prayer roll by rolling a dice. On a 1, this model suffers 1 mortal wound and the prayer is not answered. On a 2, the prayer is not answered. On a 3+, the prayer is answered.

Dance of Doom: If this prayer is answered, in the combat phase, after this model has fought in that phase for the first time, when it is your turn to pick a unit to fight, this model can be picked to fight for a second time if it is within 3" of any enemy units.

Rune of Khaine: If this prayer is answered, until your next hero phase, this model's Blade of Khaine has a Damage characteristic of D3 instead of 1.

Touch of Death: If this prayer is answered, pick 1 enemy unit within 3" of this model. Then, take a dice and hide it in one of your hands. Your opponent must pick one of your hands. If they pick the one holding the dice, that enemy unit suffers D3 mortal wounds.

COMMAND ABILITY

Orgy of Slaughter: *The Slaughter Queen orders her warriors to renew their assault twice over.*

You can use this command ability once per turn in your hero phase. If you do so, pick 1 friendly **DAUGHTERS OF KHAINE** unit that has not fought in that phase and is wholly within 12" of this model and within 3" of any enemy units. That unit can fight.

KEYWORDS ORDER, AELF, DAUGHTERS OF KHAINE, HERO, PRIEST, SLAUGHTER QUEEN

The terrifying Slaughter Queens of the Khainite cult do their worship upon the battlefield, carving a bloody furrow through the ranks of the enemy with twin deathswords as they scream their praises to the Bloody-Handed God.

• WARSCROLL •

WITCH AELVES

Witch Aelves are devotees of bloodshed and murder. Relying upon speed and dexterity over armour, they dash into combat, slashing at the enemy with zealous abandon. As fresh gore splatters across their skin, they enter a terrible and divine battle frenzy.

MELEE WEAPONS	Range	Attacks	To Hit	To Wound	Rend	Damage
Sacrificial Knife or Knives	1"	2	3+	4+	-	1

DESCRIPTION

A unit of Witch Aelves has any number of models. The unit is armed with 1 of the following weapon options: Sacrificial Knife and Bladed Buckler; or paired Sacrificial Knives.

HAG: 1 model in this unit can be a Hag. Add 1 to the Attacks characteristic of that model's melee weapons.

STANDARD BEARER: 1 in every 5 models in this unit can be a Standard Bearer. You can re-roll failed battleshock tests for units that include any Standard Bearers.

HORNBLOWER: 1 in every 5 models in this unit can be a Hornblower. Units that include any Hornblowers can run and still charge later in the same turn.

ABILITIES

Bladed Bucklers: *The martial skill of these warriors allows them to turn defensive techniques into deadly strikes.*

Add 1 to save rolls for attacks made with melee weapons that target a unit armed with Bladed Bucklers. In addition, if the unmodified save roll for an attack made with a melee weapon that targets a unit armed with Bladed Bucklers is 6, the attacking unit suffers 1 mortal wound after all of its attacks have been resolved.

Frenzied Fervour: *With their lieges nearby, Witch Aelves hurl themselves at the enemy with no fear of death.*

Add 1 to wound rolls for attacks made with melee weapons by this unit while it is wholly within 12" of any friendly **DAUGHTERS OF KHAINE HEROES.**

Paired Sacrificial Knives: *Those who carry two sacrificial knives use parries and deflections to overwhelm their foes.*

Add 1 to the Attacks characteristic of a Sacrificial Knife for models armed with a pair of Sacrificial Knives.

KEYWORDS ORDER, AELF, DAUGHTERS OF KHAINE, WITCH AELVES

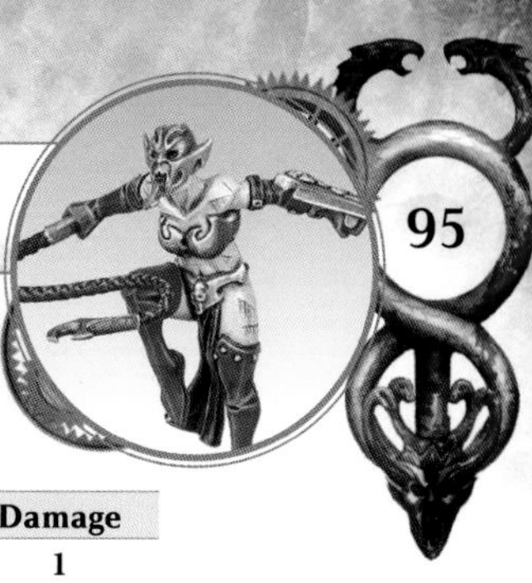

• WARSCROLL •

SISTERS OF SLAUGHTER

With skills honed in ritual duels and gladiatorial fights, the Sisters of Slaughter send their barbed whips lashing out to tear open throats and strip flesh from bone, exulting in the perfection of each gory kill.

MELEE WEAPONS	Range	Attacks	To Hit	To Wound	Rend	Damage
Barbed Whip	2"	2	3+	4+	-	1
Sacrificial Knife	1"	1	3+	4+	-	1

DESCRIPTION

A unit of Sisters of Slaughter has any number of models. The unit is armed with 1 of the following weapon options: Barbed Whip and Sacrificial Knife; or Barbed Whip and Bladed Buckler.

HANDMAIDEN: 1 model in this unit can be a Handmaiden. Add 1 to the Attacks characteristic of that model's melee weapons.

STANDARD BEARER: 1 in every 5 models in this unit can be a Standard Bearer. You can re-roll failed battleshock tests for units that include any Standard Bearers.

HORNBLOWER: 1 in every 5 models in this unit can be a Hornblower. Units that include any Hornblowers can run and still charge later in the same turn.

ABILITIES

Dance of Death: *Sisters of Slaughter manoeuvre through enemy ranks with the greatest of ease.*

This unit is eligible to fight in the combat phase if it is within 6" of an enemy unit instead of 3", and it can move an extra 3" when it piles in.

Bladed Bucklers: *The martial skill of these warriors allows them to turn defensive techniques into deadly strikes.*

Add 1 to save rolls for attacks made with melee weapons that target a unit armed with Bladed Bucklers. In addition, if the unmodified save roll for an attack made with a melee weapon that targets a unit armed with Bladed Bucklers is 6, the attacking unit suffers 1 mortal wound after all of its attacks have been resolved.

KEYWORDS ORDER, AELF, DAUGHTERS OF KHAINE, SISTERS OF SLAUGHTER

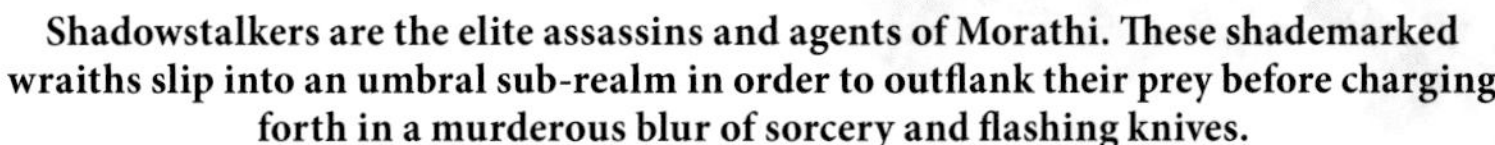

• WARSCROLL •

KHAINITE SHADOWSTALKERS

Shadowstalkers are the elite assassins and agents of Morathi. These shademarked wraiths slip into an umbral sub-realm in order to outflank their prey before charging forth in a murderous blur of sorcery and flashing knives.

MISSILE WEAPONS	Range	Attacks	To Hit	To Wound	Rend	Damage
Cursed Missiles	6"	1	4+	3+	-	1
MELEE WEAPONS	**Range**	**Attacks**	**To Hit**	**To Wound**	**Rend**	**Damage**
Assassin's Blades	1"	2	4+	3+	-	1
Umbral Blades	1"	3	3+	3+	-1	D3

DESCRIPTION

A unit of Khainite Shadowstalkers has any number of models, each armed with Cursed Missiles and Assassin's Blades.

SHROUD QUEEN: 1 model in this unit can be a Shroud Queen. A Shroud Queen is armed with Umbral Blades and Cursed Missiles. In addition, a Shroud Queen has a Wounds characteristic of 3.

ABILITIES

Shadow Leap: *Shadowstalkers can vanish and reappear at will as they navigate the Umbral Web.*

In your movement phase, instead of making a normal move with this unit, you can say that it will shadow leap. If you do so, remove this unit from the battlefield and set it up again anywhere on the battlefield more than 9" from any enemy units.

Cursed Missiles: *The slightest scratch from these weapons can spell the end of any foe.*

If the unmodified hit roll for an attack made with Cursed Missiles is 6, that attack inflicts 1 mortal wound on the target and the attack sequence ends (do not make a wound or save roll).

Harness Shadow: *Given their control of shadow itself, these assassins are almost impossible to strike.*

Subtract 1 from hit rolls for attacks made with melee weapons that target this unit.

KEYWORDS ORDER, AELF, DAUGHTERS OF KHAINE, KHAINITE SHADOWSTALKERS

• WARSCROLL •

DOOMFIRE WARLOCKS

Doomfire Warlocks are expert light cavalry, adept at harrying flanks with crossbow fire or cutting down targets with their cursed scimitars. As warlocks, they can harness the power of shadow, hurling bolts of black flame to destroy their targets.

MISSILE WEAPONS	Range	Attacks	To Hit	To Wound	Rend	Damage
Doomfire Crossbow	12"	2	4+	3+	-	1
MELEE WEAPONS	**Range**	**Attacks**	**To Hit**	**To Wound**	**Rend**	**Damage**
Cursed Scimitar	1"	2	4+	3+	-1	1
Vicious Bite	1"	2	4+	4+	-	1

DESCRIPTION

A unit of Doomfire Warlocks has any number of model, each armed with a Doomfire Crossbow and Cursed Scimitar.

MOUNT: This unit's Dark Steeds attack with their Vicious Bite.

MASTER OF WARLOCKS: 1 model in this unit can be a Master of Warlocks. Add 1 to the Attacks characteristic of that model's melee weapons.

ABILITIES

Doomfire Coven: *The arcane power of a Doomfire Coven grows with every warlock that joins their party.*

Add 1 to casting and unbinding rolls for this unit while it has 5 or more models.

MAGIC

This unit is a **WIZARD**. It can attempt to cast 1 spell in your hero phase and attempt to unbind 1 spell in the enemy hero phase. It knows the Arcane Bolt, Mystic Shield and Doomfire spells. It cannot attempt to cast any spells other than Arcane Bolt, Mystic Shield and Doomfire.

Doomfire: *The Doomfire Warlocks hurl bolts of blazing black flame at their foes.*

Doomfire has a casting value of 6. If successfully cast, pick 1 enemy unit within 12" of the casting unit and visible to it. If the casting unit has fewer than 5 models, that enemy unit suffers D3 mortal wounds. If the casting unit has between 5 and 9 models, that enemy unit suffers D6 mortal wounds. If the casting unit has 10 or more models, that enemy unit suffers 6 mortal wounds.

KEYWORDS	ORDER, AELF, DAUGHTERS OF KHAINE, WIZARD, DOOMFIRE WARLOCKS

The warriors of a Scáthcoven launch an outraged assault upon the Beasts of Chaos that have dared to stray into their subterranean domain, delighting in every agonising death they inflict on the hated creatures.

• WARSCROLL •

AVATAR OF KHAINE

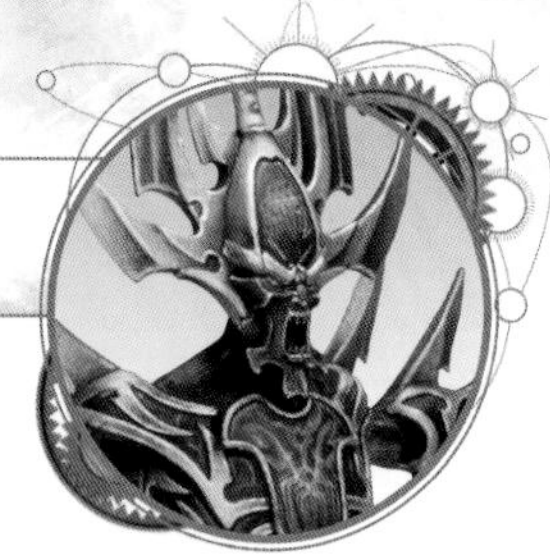

Brazen statues given animus by sorcery and sacrifice, the Avatars of Khaine stride out to fight the enemies of the Daughters of Khaine, hewing down foes with their blades or engulfing them in jets of boiling blood.

MISSILE WEAPONS	Range	Attacks	To Hit	To Wound	Rend	Damage
Torrent of Burning Blood	10"	6	3+	3+	-1	1
MELEE WEAPONS	**Range**	**Attacks**	**To Hit**	**To Wound**	**Rend**	**Damage**
Avatar's Sword	2"	4	3+	3+	-2	3

DESCRIPTION

An Avatar of Khaine is a single model armed with a Torrent of Burning Blood and Avatar's Sword.

ABILITIES

Altar of Khaine: *Prayers chanted near these idols are empowered instantly.*

Add 1 to prayer rolls for friendly **DAUGHTERS OF KHAINE PRIESTS** while they are wholly within 9" of any friendly models with this ability.

Idol of Worship: *Avatars of Khaine inspire the warrior cults of the Murder God to unleash their relentless potential.*

Add 1 to the Bravery characteristic of friendly **DAUGHTERS OF KHAINE** units while they are wholly within 12" of any friendly models with this ability.

Wrath of Khaine: *Khaine's subjects channel their faith through bladed idols of the Murder God.*

If your army includes any **AVATARS OF KHAINE**, friendly **DAUGHTERS OF KHAINE PRIESTS** can chant the following prayer.

Animated: Pick 1 friendly **AVATAR OF KHAINE** on the battlefield. Until your next hero phase, that **AVATAR OF KHAINE** is animated.

This model cannot move and cannot attack with its Torrent of Burning Blood or Avatar's Sword unless it is animated.

KEYWORDS ORDER, DAUGHTERS OF KHAINE, TOTEM, AVATAR OF KHAINE

An Avatar of Khaine is imposing enough when it simply looms over the battlefield, but when given terrible motion by the prayers of a Hag Queen or Slaughter Queen, it becomes a truly terrifying embodiment of carnage, hacking and slicing all before it into ribbons.

• WARSCROLL •

BLOOD SISTERS

Blood Sisters are Melusai, true daughters of the Shadow Queen. Channelling the hatred within their own tainted souls, each longs to drive their heartshard glaive deep into an enemy's vitals or to transmute flesh with their agonising scáth touch.

MELEE WEAPONS	Range	Attacks	To Hit	To Wound	Rend	Damage
Heartshard Glaive	2"	3	3+	3+	-1	1

DESCRIPTION

A unit of Blood Sisters has any number of models, each armed with a Heartshard Glaive.

GORGAI: 1 model in this unit can be a Gorgai. Add 1 to the Attacks characteristic of that model's Heartshard Glaive.

ABILITIES

Turned to Crystal: *The scáth touch of a Blood Sister can permanently transmute an enemy into an immobile – though still fully conscious – crystal statue.*

At the end of the combat phase, you can pick 1 enemy unit within 1" of this unit and roll 1 dice for each model in this unit. For each 3+, that enemy unit suffers 1 mortal wound.

KEYWORDS ORDER, DAUGHTERS OF KHAINE, MELUSAI, BLOOD SISTERS

• WARSCROLL •

BLOOD STALKERS

Drawing their ornate bows, the Blood Stalkers loose volleys of arrows that seek out their target's heart with uncanny accuracy. In close combat, they wield cruel curved blades, opening throats and carving out organs to offer in grisly sacrifice to Morathi.

MISSILE WEAPONS	Range	Attacks	To Hit	To Wound	Rend	Damage
Heartseeker Bow	24"	2	3+	3+	-1	1
MELEE WEAPONS	**Range**	**Attacks**	**To Hit**	**To Wound**	**Rend**	**Damage**
Scianlar	1"	2	3+	4+	-	1
Blood Wyrm	1"	1	3+	3+	-	1

DESCRIPTION

A unit of Blood Stalkers has any number of models, each armed with a Heartseeker Bow and Scianlar.

KRONE: 1 model in this unit can be a Krone. A Krone is armed with a Blood Wyrm in addition to its other weapons.

ABILITIES

Heartseekers: *The blood-blessed arrows loosed by these Melusai unerringly seek out the enemy's vital organs.*

If the unmodified hit roll for an attack made with a Heartseeker Bow is 6, that attack inflicts 1 mortal wound on the target and the attack sequence ends (do not make a wound or save roll).

KEYWORDS ORDER, DAUGHTERS OF KHAINE, MELUSAI, BLOOD STALKERS

• WARSCROLL •

KHINERAI LIFETAKERS

Khinerai Lifetakers are swift-attack specialists, elite ambushers that swoop into battle to scythe down foes with their barbed sickles. They rake enemy formations in combat before flying out of the melee to seek other vulnerable prey.

MELEE WEAPONS	Range	Attacks	To Hit	To Wound	Rend	Damage
Barbed Sickle	1"	2	3+	4+	-	1

DESCRIPTION

A unit of Khinerai Lifetakers has any number of models, each armed with a Barbed Sickle.

FLY: This unit can fly.

HARRIDYNN: 1 model in this unit can be a Harridynn. Add 1 to the Attacks characteristic of that model's weapons.

ABILITIES

Death on the Wind: *Lifetakers achieve terrifying speeds on the charge that devastate enemy ranks.*

Add 1 to the Damage characteristic of this unit's Barbed Sickles and improve the Rend characteristic of that weapon by 1 if this unit made a charge move in the same turn.

Descend to Battle: *The Khinerai delight in using their leathery wings to descend upon the foe from unexpected vectors.*

Instead of setting up this unit on the battlefield, you can place it to one side and say that it is circling high above as a reserve unit. If you do so, at the end of your movement phase, you can set up this unit on the battlefield more than 9" from any enemy units. At the start of the fourth battle round, any models that are still in reserve are slain.

Fight and Flight: *The cults of the Khinerai are masters of the hit-and-run strike.*

Each time this unit fights, you can roll a dice after all of its attacks have been resolved. On a 4+, this unit can make a retreat move of 6" (it cannot run).

Heartpiercer Shield: *The bladed shields of the Khinerai are deadly close-quarters weapons in their own right.*

Add 1 to save rolls for attacks made with melee weapons that target this unit. In addition, if the unmodified save roll for an attack made with a melee weapon that targets this unit is 6, the attacking unit suffers 1 mortal wound after all of its attacks have been resolved.

KEYWORDS ORDER, DAUGHTERS OF KHAINE, KHINERAI HARPIES, KHINERAI LIFETAKERS

• WARSCROLL •

KHINERAI HEARTRENDERS

The Khinerai Heartrenders are merciless sky-predators that scan the battlefield for suitable quarry. Should they find a target to their liking, they will streak down from on high, hurling barbed javelins and slashing with cruel heartpiercer shields.

MISSILE WEAPONS	Range	Attacks	To Hit	To Wound	Rend	Damage
Barbed Javelin	12"	1	3+	3+	-1	1
MELEE WEAPONS	**Range**	**Attacks**	**To Hit**	**To Wound**	**Rend**	**Damage**
Barbed Javelin	2"	1	4+	4+	-1	1

DESCRIPTION

A unit of Khinerai Heartrenders has any number of models, each armed with a Barbed Javelin.

FLY: This unit can fly.

SHRYKE: 1 model in this unit can be a Shryke. Add 1 to the Attacks characteristic of that model's weapons.

ABILITIES

Death From Above: *A Heartrender that has picked up sufficient momentum is capable of hurling their javelin with terrifying force.*

This unit can run and still shoot later in the same turn. In addition, improve the Rend characteristic of this unit's Barbed Javelins by 1 if this unit was set up on the battlefield in the same turn.

Descend to Battle: *The Khinerai delight in using their leathery wings to descend upon the foe from unexpected vectors.*

Instead of setting up this unit on the battlefield, you can place it to one side and say that it is circling high above as a reserve unit. If you do so, at the end of your movement phase, you can set up this unit on the battlefield more than 9" from any enemy units. At the start of the fourth battle round, any models that are still in reserve are slain.

Fire and Flight: *Heartrenders are masters of the hit-and-run strike, loosing volleys of sharpened projectiles before darting away.*

In your shooting phase, after this unit shoots, you can roll a dice. If you do so, on a 4+, this unit can make a normal move of 6" (it cannot retreat or run).

Heartpiercer Shield: *The bladed shields of the Khinerai are deadly close-quarters weapons in their own right.*

Add 1 to save rolls for attacks made with melee weapons that target this unit. In addition, if the unmodified save roll for an attack made with a melee weapon that targets this unit is 6, the attacking unit suffers 1 mortal wound after all of its attacks have been resolved.

KEYWORDS	ORDER, DAUGHTERS OF KHAINE, KHINERAI HARPIES, KHINERAI HEARTRENDERS

• ENDLESS SPELL WARSCROLL •

BLOODWRACK VIPER

The Bloodwrack Viper is an enormous serpent formed from boiling blood, a manifestation of hatred and bitterness that binds its prey in a crushing embrace before squeezing so forcefully that the victim explodes in a shower of gore.

DESCRIPTION

A Bloodwrack Viper is a single model.

PREDATORY: A Bloodwrack Viper is a predatory endless spell. It can move up to 9" and can fly.

MAGIC

Summon Bloodwrack Viper: *The caster weaves their outstretched hand in an elaborate pattern that mimics the structure of a monstrous snake drenched in blood.*

Summon Bloodwrack Viper has a casting value of 7. Only **Daughters of Khaine Wizards** can attempt to cast this spell. If successfully cast, set up 1 Bloodwrack Viper model wholly within 9" of the caster.

ABILITIES

Bloodslick Coils: *The viper uses the torrents of blood from its scales to slide at great speed.*

When this model is set up, the player who set it up can immediately make a move with it.

Fanged Strike: *The serpent curls around its enemies and tightens its coils, choking its prey in torrents of unnatural ichor before striking with its monstrous fangs.*

After this model has moved, the player who moved this endless spell must pick 1 unit within 1" of it and roll 3 dice. For each roll that is equal to or greater than that unit's Wounds characteristic, 1 model from that unit is slain.

KEYWORDS	ENDLESS SPELL, BLOODWRACK VIPER

• ENDLESS SPELL WARSCROLL •

BLADEWIND

Carried through the air by a crimson tempest of blood, these gleaming falchions carve a bloody path through anything in their way, slicing through armour with unnatural ease to get to the flesh and blood beneath.

DESCRIPTION

Bladewind is a single model.

PREDATORY: Bladewind is a predatory endless spell. It can move up to 12" and can fly.

MAGIC

Summon Bladewind: *The caster calls upon their mastery of blood magic to conjure a twirling quartet of giant, blood-slick blades.*

Summon Bladewind has a casting value of 6. Only **Daughters of Khaine Wizards** can attempt to cast this spell. If successfully cast, set up 1 Bladewind model wholly within 9" of the caster.

ABILITIES

Eviscerating Vortex: *Upon taking form, these sentient blades simultaneously begin to spin at an alarming rate.*

When this model is set up, the player who set it up can immediately make a move with it.

Unnatural Edge: *The falchions carve through rock and masonry effortlessly, preying on those who would seek shelter behind them.*

After this model has moved, each unit that has any models it passed across, and each other unit that is within 1" of it at the end of its move, suffers D3 mortal wounds.

In addition, do not apply the cover modifier to save rolls for attacks that target units that are within 12" of this model.

KEYWORDS	ENDLESS SPELL, BLADEWIND

HEART OF FURY

The most devout of Khaine's priestesses can summon a manifestation of his Iron Heart, a blood-dripping icon that burns with supernatural rage. Those bathed in its wrathful aura continue to fight and kill even when stricken with mortal wounds.

DESCRIPTION

A Heart of Fury is a single model.

A Heart of Fury is not set up on the battlefield at the start of the game. Instead, a **Daughters of Khaine Priest** from your army can summon it to the battlefield by making an invocation roll (see opposite).

Unless noted otherwise, a Heart of Fury cannot be attacked or affected by spells or abilities; it is treated as a friendly model by all armies for any other rules purposes. In order to attempt to summon a Heart of Fury, you must have a model available that is not already in your army and on the battlefield. A Heart of Fury cannot be attempted to be summoned more than once per turn. A Heart of Fury has a Pitched Battle profile and a points cost.

INVOCATION OF KHAINE

Summon Heart of Fury: *The skies turn crimson as this bleeding icon descends upon the battle.*

In your hero phase, 1 friendly **Daughters of Khaine Priest** can attempt to summon this invocation. If they do so, make a invocation roll by rolling a dice. On a 3+, the invocation roll is successful. If the invocation roll is successful, set up this model wholly within 12" of that **Daughters of Khaine Priest**.

ABILITIES

Locus of the Murder God: *This prayer takes the form of Khaine's undying power and bestows death-defying energies upon his faithful.*

Subtract 1 from the damage inflicted (to a minimum of 1) by each successful attack that targets a **Daughters of Khaine** unit wholly within 12" of this model.

Pledge to Khaine: *Devotion must be maintained for this icon of worship to remain alongside its Khainite subjects.*

At the end of each battle round, if this model is on the battlefield, the player who set up this model must roll a dice. Add 1 to the roll if there are any **Avatars of Khaine** within 6" of this model. On a 1-3, this model is removed from the battlefield.

KEYWORDS	INVOCATION OF KHAINE, HEART OF FURY

Clenched in a fist of iron, a brazen Heart of Fury is a potent manifestation of Khainite faith. More terrifying still are the spells favoured by Morathi's sorcerers: the gore-dripping serpent known as a Bloodwrack Viper and the whirling vortex of swords they call the Bladewind.

PITCHED BATTLE PROFILES

The table below provides points, minimum and maximum unit sizes and battlefield roles for the warscrolls and warscroll battalions in this book, for use in Pitched Battles. Spending the points listed on this table allows you to take a minimum-sized unit with any of its upgrades. Understrength units cost the full amount of points. Larger units are taken in multiples of their minimum unit size; multiply their cost by the same amount as you multiplied their size. If a unit has two points values separated by a slash (e.g. '60/200'), the second value is for a maximum-sized unit. Units that are listed as 'Unique' are named characters and can only be taken once in an army. A unit that has any of the keywords listed on the Allies table can be taken as an allied unit by a Daughters of Khaine army. Updated February 2021; the profiles printed here take precedence over any profiles with an earlier publication date or no publication date.

DAUGHTERS OF KHAINE WARSCROLL	UNIT SIZE MIN	UNIT SIZE MAX	POINTS	BATTLEFIELD ROLE	NOTES
Sisters of Slaughter	10	30	120	Battleline	
Witch Aelves	10	30	100	Battleline	
Avatar of Khaine	1	1	130	Behemoth	
Bloodwrack Medusa	1	1	100	Leader	
Hag Queen	1	1	90	Leader	
Melusai Ironscale	1	1	110	Leader	
Morathi-Khaine	1	1	210	Leader	Unique. These units must be taken as a set for a total of 600 points. Although taken as a set, each is a separate unit.
The Shadow Queen	1	1	390	Leader, Behemoth	
Morgwaeth the Bloodied	1	1	80	Leader	Unique. These units must be taken as a set for a total of 80 points. Although taken as a set, each is a separate unit.
The Blade-coven	4	4			
Slaughter Queen	1	1	100	Leader	
Bloodwrack Shrine	1	1	160	Leader, Behemoth	
Hag Queen on Cauldron of Blood	1	1	220	Leader, Behemoth	
Slaughter Queen on Cauldron of Blood	1	1	270	Leader, Behemoth	
Blood Sisters	5	20	130		Battleline if general is a **BLOODWRACK MEDUSA** or **MELUSAI IRONSCALE**
Blood Stalkers	5	20	140		Battleline if general is a **BLOODWRACK MEDUSA** or **MELUSAI IRONSCALE**
Doomfire Warlocks	5	20	120		
Khainite Shadowstalkers	9	18	100		
Khinerai Heartrenders	5	20	80		
Khinerai Lifetakers	5	20	80		
Cauldron Guard	-	-	*120*	*Warscroll Battalion*	
Scáthcoven	-	-	*140*	*Warscroll Battalion*	
Shadow Patrol	-	-	*130*	*Warscroll Battalion*	
Shrine Brood	-	-	*120*	*Warscroll Battalion*	
Slaughter Troupe	-	-	*130*	*Warscroll Battalion*	
Vyperic Guard	-	-	*140*	*Warscroll Battalion*	
War Coven of Morathi	-	-	*100*	*Warscroll Battalion*	
Bladewind	*1*	*1*	*40*	*Endless Spell*	
Bloodwrack Viper	*1*	*1*	*40*	*Endless Spell*	
Heart of Fury	*1*	*1*	*80*	*Invocation of Khaine*	*Unique*

FACTION	ALLIES
Daughters of Khaine	Cities of Sigmar, Idoneth Deepkin